The Valmiki
RAMAYANA
Retold in Verse

Volume II

The Valmiki
RAMAYANA
Retold in Verse
Volume II

SWAMI RAMA

THE HIMALAYAN INTERNATIONAL INSTITUTE
OF YOGA SCIENCE AND PHILOSOPHY
OF THE U.S.A.
HONESDALE, PENNSYLVANIA

Himalayan International Institute
of Yoga Science and Philosophy of the U.S.A.
RR 1, Box 400
Honesdale, PA 18431-9706

First Printing 1993

The paper used in this publication meets the minimum
requirements of American National Standard for
Information Sciences Permanence of Paper for Printed
Library Materials, ANSI Z39.48-1984. ⊗

Hard ISBN 0-89389-138-x
Paper ISBN 0-89389-139-8

CONTENTS—VOLUME II

INTRODUCTION TO MAIN CHARACTERS

In the *Ramayana*, many characters have titles or alternative names that reflect part of their role or their relationships to others. Rama, the hero of the epic, is known by several special titles or designations, for example, "Best of Men", as well as Ramchandra, Raghav and other names. Sita, Ram's wife is known as Vaidehi (daughter of Videha) or Maithili (from the region her father ruled). To help the modern reader enjoy this epic poem, the following summary of the main characters and their alternative names is provided.

BHARAT, (BHARATA). Ram's younger brother, son of Dasharatha and Kaikeyi, a partial incarnation of Vishnu.

BIBHISHAN. A rakshasa, younger brother of Ravan. He became King of Lanka after Ravan's death.

DASHARATHA. The King of Ayodhya, father of Ram, Bharat, Lakshman, and Shatrughan. Also known as Kakutstha.

HANUMAN. The son of the Wind God and nymph Anjana. A banar warrior, friend of Sugriva and devotee of Ram, who helped Ram locate Sita.

INDRA. The King of the Gods. Also known as Devendra.

INDRAJIT. A rakshasa, son of Ravan, vanquisher of Indra, also known as Meghanad.

JANAK (JANAKA). The King of Mithila, father of Sita, also known as Videha.

JAṬĀYU. The King of Birds, friend of Dasharatha.

KAIKEYI. One of King Dasharatha's queens, mother of Bharat.

KAUSHALYA. One of King Dasharatha's queens, mother of Ram.

LAKSHMAN (LAKSHMANA). Younger brother of Ram and Bharat, son of Dasharatha and Sumitra, a partial incarnation of Vishnu.

RAM (RAMA). An avatar of Vishnu. Son of Dasharatha and Kaushalya, older brother of Lakshman, Bharat, and Shatrughan. Also known as Sri Ram, Raghav, Kakutstha, Raghunanda, Ramachandra, Best of Men, and Joy of the House of Raghu.

RAVAN (RAVANA). A rakshasa and King of Titans. Also known as Dashanana.

SHATRUGHAN. The youngest brother of Ram, twin brother of Lakshman, son of Dasharatha and Sumitra. A partial incarnation of Vishnu.

SITA. Consort of Ram, daughter of King Janak. Also known as Janaki, Vaidehi, Maithili. A divine incarnation of Lakshmi.

SUGRIVA. King of Banars and younger brother of Bali.

VAISHRAVANA. The Guardian of Wealth, brother of Ravan, son of Vishrava. Also known as Dashana.

VALMIKI. The sage who composed the poems of the Ramayana.

VASHISHTHA. A divine sage and family priest of Dasharatha.

VISHRAVA. The son of the divine sage Pulastya and father of Vaishravana and Ravan.

VISHWAMITRA. A sage who attained brahminhood through austerity and taught Ram the use of divine weapons.

EDITOR'S NOTE

We have used the diacritical marks only on selected Sanskrit words. The rationale behind the limited use of these marks is to help readers pronounce key terms as accurately as possible without making the text academic and overly technical. Thus, only the terms that are likely to be mispronounced by English-speaking readers or those that may convey a different meaning to those who have some knowledge of Sanskrit carry diacritical marks. For example, without diacritical marks, the word "kāṇḍa," can be mispronounced. It also has an entirely different meaning. In this particular text, "kāṇḍa," means "canto" or "chapter," whereas, "kanda" means "root." (Generally, kanda means edible roots although in kundalini yoga literature, it refers to *muladhara*.)

We have not used the diacritical marks with proper nouns that are still in vogue in Hindi or other Indian languages and which are used frequently in English. We have used diacritical marks with those proper nouns that are no longer commonly used or which might convey the wrong meaning if written without diacriticals.

Above all, we invite the reader to simply enjoy the poetry and rhythm of the verses as well as the beauty of the story being told.

Pronunciation of Sanskrit Words

a	org*a*n, s*u*m
ā	*fa*ther
ai	*ai*sle
au	s*au*erkr*au*t
b	*b*ut
bh	a*bh*or
ch	*ch*ur*ch*
chh	chur*chh*ill
ḍ	*d*ough
d	*d*ough (slightly toward the *th* sound of *th*ough)

ḍh	a*dh*ere
dh	a*dh*ere (slightly toward the *theh* sound of brea*the h*ere)
e	pr*ey*
g	*g*o
gh	do*gh*ouse
h	*h*ot
i	*i*t
ī	pol*i*ce
j	*j*ump
jh	lod*ge*house
k	*k*id
kh	wor*kh*orse
l	*l*ug
m	*m*ud
ṇ	u*n*der
n	*n*o
o	n*o*
p	*p*ub
p	u*ph*ill
r	*r*um
sh	*sh*un
s	*s*un
ṭ	*t*omato
t	wa*t*er
ṭh	an*th*ill
th	*Th*ailand
u	p*u*sh
ū	r*u*de
v	*v*odka (midway between *w* and *v*)
y	*y*es

Sundara Kāṇḍa

SUNDARA KĀṆḌA is the description of Lanka, Ravana's capital. Hanuman flies across the ocean to Lanka, searching for Sita in the capital and palace of Ravana. He finds her sitting alone under a tree in the Ashoka Grove, guarded by female demons. Ravana comes to the grove to persuade Sita to marry him, but she refuses. Ravana threatens to give her only two more months to live. Sita laments. After being left alone, Sita talks with Hanuman. He wants to rescue her, but Sita wishes to be rescued only by Rama. Sita gives Hanuman one of her jewels as a token for Rama. Hanuman burns the fortress of Lanka and slays many of Ravana's warriors. He allows himself to be bound by the rope of Brahma and is taken before Ravana. Hanuman escapes and sets fire to all of Lanka. He takes leave of Sita and returns to the banars waiting for him on the other shore. Hanuman reports to Sugriva, Rama and Lakshman that he has found Sita.

Sundara Kāṇḍa

1

With homage unto every god,
Hanuman the mountain trod.
Assuming a gigantic shape,
The banars stood with mouths agape.
He stretched his neck and wagged his tail
And all the banars did him hail.
The mountain pressed beneath his feet,
Streams and serpents did secrete.
The blossoms from the trees did rain,
Carpeting the rough terrain.
Serpents found within the cave,
Raised their hoods and tails did wave
As from their mouths great flames did spit,
And their venom did emit.
The rishis and the devas ran
When Hanuman assumed his plan.
The siddhas in the spacious sky
Witnessed him prepare to fly.
Hanuman did roar and quiver,
Causing all who watched to shiver.
Then he crouched before he leapt;
In breathless silence all were kept
As he darted into space,

Like a bullet out of place.
As Hanuman through space did speed,
He told the banars there to heed,
That Sita would by him be borne
Or all of Lanka would be torn.
By the force with which he leapt,
The shrubs and trees in space were swept.
His eyes revealed a hidden glow
As fire beneath the ember show.
Of copper hue and brilliant eyes,
That banar like the thunder flies.
As that banar coursed through space,
The ocean he did soon displace.
The waves as mountains were upheaved
As swiftly through the air he cleaved.
The animals within the sea
Were churned as Hanuman did spree.
For miles his shadow cast a veil
Like a deep aquatic whale.
With his hands he pushed aside
Those clouds that on his path did ride.
Flowers from the sky did shower
When they saw that banar's power.
The ocean thought he should support
Hanuman in his purport.
Maināka, the mountain crest,
He told to rise at his behest,
To offer rest unto that ranger,
To his mission not endanger.
Underneath, Maināka stood,
The nether regions he withstood.
Devendra wished to post him there
So asuras would beware.
Now the ocean did request
That mountain to provide him rest.
From the ocean he emerged,

His crests, which had been there submerged.
Like a golden pinnacle,
He glistened like an oracle,
Reaching high into the sky
To offer rest as he did fly.
Hanuman the mountain saw,
Its beauty filling all with awe.
An obstacle is what he thought,
To hinder him, the mountain sought.
With his chest he broke its crest
And by the siddhas he was blest.
Maināka enjoyed his fun,
This prowess of the Wind God's son.
As a human he did stand,
Maināka bestowed his hand:
"Oh Great Ranger of the Trees,
Pause a while and take your ease.
The House of Raghu sired the sea,
He offers you felicity.
To serve the heir of Raghu's race,
He offers you a resting place.
Feast upon these fruits and roots,
Before resuming your pursuits.
By Sagar has the sea been born,
By fatigue you have been worn,
So the Sea God offers thee
His blessings and prosperity.
Oh Best of Banars, please do heed,
And take from us what you do need.
To honor you in this small way
I can your sire a debt repay.
Long ago when we had wings,
The mountains coursed the air like kings.
Rishis soon became afraid
That we would to the earth cascade.
Devendra cruelly wings did sever;

Now we are earthbound forever.
When Devendra raised his mace,
The wind my mighty form did place
Far into the salty sea
Where the ocean shelters me.
Oh Hanuman, I thee adore,
Because of aught thy sire before.
Thy father did protect my wing,
His glory from my lips does sing.
Grant us this auspicious grace,
Thou who serves the Raghu race."
Hanuman before avowed
No obstacle would be allowed,
And neither would he pause or rest
Until he had fulfilled his quest.
He blessed the mountain with his hand
And then proceeded as he planned.
The devas did applaud this feat
And offered praise both kind and sweet.
Maināka they also praised,
His selfless act had them amazed.
Devendra did the mountain bless
For this act of fearlessness.
Indra did a blessing give
That Maināka could freely live.
Hanuman did swiftly fly
Through the vast, expansive sky.
The devas did arrange a test
To hinder him upon his quest.
Sursa, Mother of the Snake,
Did a demon's form betake.
From the depth she did arise,
Venomous with copper eyes.
On his path she blocked his way,
And had these fearful words to say:
"Brahma's boon I did receive

That none can from me pass or leave
Until my mouth you enter here;
To this boon you must adhere.
For food you have become my fare,
So enter now and have no care."
Hanuman explained his mission
Failing to give her submission,
Promising he would return,
To honor that which she did earn.
Defiantly had Sursa said,
First she would be duly fed.
Hanuman to her retorted
As if with a child he sported,
Open high and wide enough
To swallow him, he did rebuff.
To forty miles she grew her jaw
And Hanuman did match her maw.
Then fifty miles again she grew
And Hanuman did match her, too.
To sixty miles her mouth did stretch
But seventy he did so fetch.
Then eighty miles her jaw grew wide
And Hanuman did ninety bide.
A hundred miles she had assumed,
Like the jaws of death she loomed.
Then Hanuman became so small,
He was only thumb-height tall.
Into her mouth he quickly sped
And just as quickly, out he fled.
Then to Sursa he did croon
That he had honored Brahma's boon.
Sursa did resume her form,
Beautiful, she did transform.
She blessed the banar to resume
The quest that did his heart illume.
All celestial beings praised

That banar Anjanā had raised.
Through the sky the banar soared,
With a speed that loudly roared.
Singhika, a wretched beast,
Set her eyes on him to feast.
She held his shadow in her grip,
Thus she did impinge his trip.
For he was by her held fast,
And she was happy now at last
To find a meal to stave her hunger,
She, a raw flesh-eating monger.
Hanuman, his size did change,
Filling all the southern range.
Singhika upon him lunged;
Her jaws agape to him expunged.
But Hanuman his form contracted,
Like a bullet he impacted
Going down that demon's throat,
Her bowels had that banar smote.
When he tore her flesh asunder,
He emerged like roaring thunder.
All the siddhas did acclaim
That banar of eternal fame.
Hanuman then reached the shore
Where none like him had gone before.
Many were the thickened wood
That on the island bravely stood.
Then Hanuman, by nature wise,
Did resume his former size.
On the top of Samva Mountain,
Blazed the city like a fountain.

2

Without fatigue the banar came
To Lanka that the seas did claim.
Petals on him then did rain

When he did the shore attain.
Through fields and valleys, fragrance-laden,
Ponds as fresh as youthful maiden;
Flowers on the treetops sway
And birds upon their boughs did play;
Hanuman then made his way
Yet his senses did not sway.
There was a moat around the city;
Lotuses did make it pretty.
Guards with weapons did surround
That golden-walled and brilliant ground.
Its palaces of brilliant light
Did illuminate the night.
Vishvakarma did construct
This city with its aqueduct.
Golden arches, spiral tower,
Did encase an evil power.
Hanuman in thought immersed,
His plan of action he rehearsed.
How could he remain unknown,
To conduct his search alone?
So he waited for the night
When the moonbeam casts its light.
And suddenly, just like a cat,
He reduced his size to that.

3

The sound of waves and ocean breezes,
High upon the mountain pleases.
Warriors did now surround
The walls and all the city ground.
With gates of gold and roads of pearl,
Where emeralds and jewels unfurl,
And bells upon the wind did jingle,
Causing Hanuman to tingle;
Swans and peacocks could be heard

As if they spoke poetic word;
So Hanuman the land surveyed,
But misgivings it conveyed.
Like a woman newly spurned,
Lanka, in her splendor, burned.
The deity that did preside
Roared and wore a monstrous hide.
Challenging the Wind God's son,
She barred the way to Hanuman.
Obedient unto her fate,
She did guard the city's gate.
None could pass or enter there,
She did guard it everywhere.
Hanuman with patience bore
Her assault and bellowed roar.
With his fist he pushed aside
That woman of the filthy hide.
Since she was a woman born,
He had chivalry foresworn.
By one thrust the devi thrown,
The strength of Hanuman was known.
Mercy from him she did seek,
Recalling what the Lord did speak.
"The moment when you are subdued,
By a banar so behooved,
The titan race will freely be
Subject to adversity."
To Hanuman she did entreat
To enter and his wishes meet.

4

The wall of Lanka then he leapt,
That banar who's in war adept.
Through the streets the banar went,
Upon his mission, still intent.
The houses tinkled with their bell,

Where chanting women, there did dwell;
And Vedic scripture was recited
Where the pandits fires ignited;
Many were the songs of praise,
For he who did the heavens raze;
Many were the spies who met
In the courtyard where they'd set;
Giants, dwarfs with matted hair,
Naked, shaven, all were there;
Warriors with weaponry,
Displayed their forms of canonry.
With rich attire and fragrant paste,
Some with one- and some two-faced,
The inner chambers they did guard,
From above and in the yard.
The palace of the king was seen
By Hanuman, in prowess keen.
Surrounded by a river moat
With lotuses, as he did note,
And song and dance from there were heard,
As well as elephants and herd.
So that banar there did pierce,
To the hall of one so fierce.

5

The full moon graced the velvet night
Illuminating all with light.
The limpid pool of darkness bore
That milky orb unto its shore.
And all upon the ground unveils
Beneath its rays, in full details.
Hanuman could clearly see
The city in entirety.
Women with their lovers slept,
As titans on their watch had crept;
Mansions bathed in luxury,

All displayed their battery;
Titans did debate desire,
Igniting each the other's ire;
And many were the courtesans,
In toiletries like artisans;
Some did worship, some gave threat,
Some were thin and some thickset;
Some in love were then embraced,
Some were modest, some were chaste.
Women of surpassing beauty,
Were rehearsed in carnal duty;
Nowhere could that banar find
The one foremost upon his mind.
The one who was from Brahma born,
That precious gems used to adorn,
Nowhere could he find a trace
Of she who did Ram's heart misplace.

6

Onto the roofs the banar leapt,
And freely in the night he crept.
Ravan's palace he beheld
In beauty quite unparalleled.
Many titans there stood guard
And for their lives had no regard.
Archways with ornate brocade,
And cushions with rare jewels were made.
Birds and deer and ponds adorn
The courtyard of that king lovelorn.
The sound of gongs and tambourine,
And conches did augment the scene.
In wealth and jewels it's unsurpassed,
Stealthily, the banar passed.
In all the houses did he spy,
From roof to roof, he was so sly.
Elephants and horses bred

For war, were kept in spacious shed.
And chariots of huge dimension,
In the moonlight glow and glisten.
Many female demons bare
Their teeth, to guard his quarters there.
Within his chambers women swayed;
Wine upon their breath was laid.

7

The banar did resume his search,
And on the window sills did perch,
Where mansions like celestial halls,
Inspire the one who on them calls.
Ravan's palace did he see
Adorned with gems exquisitely.
Then his chariot he found;
Through the worlds it was renowned.
Pushpak was its honored name
Whose beauty did the world acclaim.
With golden birds and silver snakes,
Elephants and glassy lakes,
The sides of that great car were sketched,
With images both carved and etched.
But still he could not find the one
Whose purity was like the sun.

8

Through the air that car did glide,
Easily through space could ride.
And Hanuman did gaze at it,
Marvelling at every bit.
Vishvakarma did construct
This marvel that its foes obstruct.
Scenes of beauty did encase
That chariot which soared through space.
Many were the rooms it bore,

Like a mountain did it soar.
With the speed of thought it flew
And all its foes with ease subdue.

9

Then Hanuman, a hall approached,
The harem of the king he broached.
Many were the soldiers hence
Adept in means of all defence.
They did guard the women fair;
None could gaze or enter there.
Some were daughters of a king
That Ravan gained through vanquishing.
Some did come and were his loves
And followed him like turtledoves.
With tapestries of golden thread,
And pearls encasing every bed,
And precious gems upon the wall,
And golden vessels, short and tall,
With emeralds and blue sapphire,
Glowing deep within with fire,
With crystal floors and balcony,
And ivory carved with artistry,
It did resemble Indra's hall,
Upon the sun it cast a pall.
Women clothed in silken dress,
Drunkenly did each caress,
And when their hair and clothes did twist,
Each unto the other kissed.
Everywhere his women lay,
Their gowns upon each one did stray.
Viands, wines, and flowers wafted
On the breeze, as down it drafted.
Jewels upon the floor did scatter,
As the night had closed their chatter.
Every woman in that place

Was endowed with beauty's grace.
Nowhere was Vaidehi found,
As Hanuman did look around.

10

Entering another room,
Where all within did wine consume,
There the King of Titans lay,
His jewels upon the bed did splay.
Hanuman in fright slipped back
As if the king did him attack.
Then he gazed upon the face
That celestial jewels did trace.
Mammoth like a mountain range,
That titan who his form could change,
Like a thundercloud he lay,
And women did his sides array.
As he slept his breath did hiss,
Fatigued from dalliance and bliss.
Dark of hue with purple tint,
His energy in lust was spent.
As the sun shoots forth its rays,
The splendor of that titan strays
Illuminating all without;
His brilliance left no one in doubt.
And those who sang and those who danced
Fell asleep where they had chanced,
Their instruments they did embrace,
As if it was their lover's face.
A bed apart from all the rest,
Adorned with gems and golden crest,
Did cradle his most favored queen,
Whose beauty none before had seen.
Hanuman jumped in delight,
Cavorting in the moonlit night;

He thought he knew where Sita stayed
Upon a bed of silk brocade.

11

But then he knew she was not there—
Sita, lost in deep despair—
And began to search once more
The chambers where he'd gone before.
The banquet hall he passed about
As he did the corners scout,
Where many foods unknown to man
Were left untouched within the pan.
Drunken women there had slept
And their wine with them was kept.
The flesh of fish and bear and hen,
Buffalo and venison,
Dressed in sauces and confection,
Gave the palate delectation.
All the women there were fair;
Some were dark with golden hair.
Yet Janaki he could not trace;
She was absent from that place.
Though to look on others' wives
Is a sin amongst the wise,
Hanuman was pure of heart;
His heart and mind were quite apart.
To other quarters did he go,
He hoped he would Vaidehi know.

12

Hanuman became discouraged,
Feeling deep inside disparaged.
Every corner did he seek
For any sign of her mystique,
But failing to find any trace,
Once again he searched this place.

But now his prowess came to nought,
And Hanuman, immersed in thought,
Reflected how he was to tell
The others what her fate befell:

13
"Many times I searched this place,
But failing to find any trace
Of that high-souled pious queen,
A sign of her I cannot glean.
Sampātī said that she was here,
But her death is what I fear.
Did she fall into the sea,
Or was devoured ruthlessly?
Or was she caged just like a bird,
Lost to us, her fate unheard?
My courage has brought me to nought,
Failing to find what I sought.
What will now Sugriva say,
Since our time it did delay?
Surely Ram would end his life
If he learned he'd lost his wife.
Lakshman soon will follow him,
And Bharat, too, will go with them.
Shatrughan will pass away;
Their mothers too will go that way.
Sugriva out of true compassion,
His own death will likewise fashion.
Then his queens will end their lives,
All of them, his faithful wives.
Angada and others, too,
Will seek the Lord of Death to woo.
Everywhere misfortune trailed,
So from them I should be veiled.
They will think there still is hope,
If I remain upon this slope.

If Janaki I fail to find,
Then I shall leave this life behind.
Or this world I shall dissolve,
Since I failed in my resolve.
Or Ravan I will bind and tie,
And through the air to Ram will fly.
Then her death will be avenged,
And satisfied, we'll be revenged.
To search for her I shall not cease;
It is the only way of peace.
Here is an Ashoka grove,
Nestled in a spacious cove.
I will search for her within
To satisfy the Best of Men.
In homage to the gods I pray,
Their blessings now on me to lay,
That I may find Prince Raghav's queen,
Confer on me the ways and mean."

14
That mountain grove, full of delight,
Was captured there in full moonlight.
Every flower could be found
Growing on that pleasant mound,
And deer and birds did there abound,
Sleeping on the trees and ground.
Where cuckoos cooed and peacocks wooed
And humming bees did change your mood,
One who did this grove behold
Was ravished by its beauty bold.
Blossoms from the trees did fall,
As Hanuman beneath did crawl.
From tree to tree the banar leapt
And all the boughs their blossoms wept.
Many were the glassy ponds,
Adorned with jewels and lacy fronds.

Waterfalls, a hidden cave,
To the grove, a magic gave.
Quietly, the banar waited;
In the tree he agitated,
For he knew that he would see
The coming of sweet Maithili.

15

Many were the birds that swayed
In golden trees with blossoms sprayed.
Ponds of crystal did reflect
The mind of that great architect.
Many were the songs of love
That birds did sing in boughs above.
Hanuman did never tire
Within this grove of keen desire.
A marble temple did he see,
Flawless in its majesty,
And titan women did surround
A woman sitting on the ground.
In dirty clothes this woman sat,
Her hair dressed in a single plat.
Her moon-like face was streaked with tears
And her mind consumed with fears.
Fasting, she had lost her glow,
Yet still her beauty one could know.
Hanuman did then surmise
This lady was Prince Raghav's prize.
Janaki, a gentle doe,
Was riven by great waves of woe.
And these demons did surround
Vaidehi like a fearful hound.
Her mind was fixed on Ram alone;
Her devotion there was shown.

16

That banar to himself did muse,
How destiny one's life does choose:
"Sita is the reason why
Many heroes past did die.
Bāli, Khara, and Virādha,
Dushana and yet Kabandha,
Many demons and their host,
Raghav did their bodies roast.
Because of her dear lotus eyes,
Sugriva did regain his prize.
Sita, born from Mother Earth,
Is equal to Prince Raghav's worth.
She followed Raghav to the wood,
Forever by his side she stood.
Now Ram is fixed on Janaki
And she on Ram eternally."
Hanuman felt sympathy;
Her plight inspired his empathy.

17

Fearless through the sky did sail
The moon, whose light did all unveil,
And Hanuman could clearly see
Vaidehi, in her misery.
Worn and tired, her beauty shorn,
Vaidehi, for her love, did mourn.
The titan women did appear
To threaten her with sword and spear.
Hairy, hairless, short and tall,
Dwarfen, hunchbacked, big and small,
One-eyed, no-eyed, earless, faceless,
Heads of goat or simply headless—
So these demons did assail
That tender bride so young and frail.
Like a flame engulfed by smoke,

Her beauty one could still evoke.
Joyfully that banar cried,
Felicity he felt inside,
And homage paid unto that One,
Resplendent like the morning sun.

18

Soon the dawn would show her face,
Impatiently that one did pace,
To get a closer look to see
The plight of peerless Janaki.
Skillful bards began to sing
The Vedas when that Titan King
Awoke and rose from out of bed,
Though wine and lust did cloud his head.
Thinking of sweet Maithili,
The king approached majestically,
Surrounded by his peerless wives,
Still drunken with their copper eyes.
The valor of that Titan King
Did illumination bring.
Raw desire consumed his mind,
As he searched the grove to find
Vaidehi of the tender limbs,
To satisfy his evil whims.
Hanuman shrank in the trees,
Blending with the boughs and leaves.

19

As Ravan did Vaidehi stalk,
With a slow and measured walk,
She trembled like a plantain leaf,
Swaying in the winds of grief.
Vaidehi did avert her gaze
As his eyes did her appraise,

And in her heart she prayed to Ram
To quickly shelter her therefrom.

20

Ravan to Vaidehi spoke
The thoughts that she did then provoke:
"Why do you so hide from me,
Your breasts and thighs so temptingly?
Patiently I for thee mourn;
My love for you has been foresworn.
The custom of the titan king—
That he, another's wife can bring—
We freely practice in this tribe,
It is a law we do ascribe.
Youth just like the river passes,
Like the sand in hourglasses.
Youth does not to one return;
My advice you should not spurn.
Why to sit upon the ground,
When next to me you could be crowned?
Wrapped in dirty clothes you sit,
This your charms does not befit.
Cast away your fears and be
Relaxed with me in luxury.
When on thee I lay my eye,
My senses do my mind belie.
All my wealth will now be yours,
My love for thee now flows and pours.
To all thy relatives I'll give
The worlds, in luxury they'll live.
Raghav, born of worthless strand,
Outcast from his home and land—
He can never me subdue;
Your fate you should no longer rue.
Now cast aside your sighs and tears,
Relinquish all your hidden fears.

Adorn thyself with precious gems
And dress thy hair in diadems.
Come with me, sit by my side;
Be my beautiful new bride."

21

A straw between them did she place
And answered as she turned her face:
"Give thy heart unto thy wives,
And meddle not in other's lives.
Of noble conduct I am born,
And to my duty I am sworn.
Your treasure cannot me entice,
The love of Ram does all suffice.
Surely you shall meet destruction
For this act of vile abduction.
Those who are oppressed will say
Your death will make them light and gay.
You should seek for Ram's alliance
And renounce your vain defiance.
For this cowardice you wielded,
Now your life to Ram is yielded."

22

Ravan harshly to her said
Words that filled his queens with dread:
"It has been said a man should be
Full of charm and chivalry.
Now I see a woman's like
A horse, that needs a whip and spike.
Harsh words spoken unto me
Warrant death with certainty.
Two months here you can abide,
Then you shall with me reside
Or my cooks will mince your flesh,
In the sauce of death to mesh."

But Sita, rich in fortitude,
To his death she did allude:
"For this insult you have rendered,
You to Ram will be surrendered.
How is it that your eyes remain,
When they gazed with thoughts profane?
Or your tongue remains intact
When threats to me it did enact?
My tapas can on thee outlash,
Reducing thee to dirty ash.
These acts will prove to your destruction,
Thou whose mind dwells on seduction."
Like a storm the titan menaced,
As in wrath his face was grimaced.
Ravan angrily did shout
Today her life he would cast out.
The female guards he did command
To use whatever means at hand,
Inducing Sita to agree
To favor him good-naturedly.
His copper eyes in anger flashed,
As his tongue his orders lashed.
A female titan did embrace
That menace of the human race,
And with her charms she swept away
That titan to his anger stay.

23

These titan women did address
Vaidehi, in her grave distress,
Praising Ravan's charms and traits,
A worthy consort her awaits.
All the devas he defeats;
There is none with him competes.
Sita as his queen would be
Worshipped in great luxury.

All the world to him does bow;
It behooves her to avow
And become his favorite queen;
Refusing could her peril mean.

24

Those demon women did harass
Vaidehi, with words harsh and crass.
They threatened to devour her limbs,
Each according to her whims,
And called to bring their fruited wine
To drink, as they did on her dine.
On Sri Ram her mind was fixed;
The hearts of both were thus transfixed.
Hanuman, atop the tree,
Witnessed Sita silently.
Janaki burst into tears
As these demons waved their spears.

25

Trembling, Sita freely wept,
Her hair and clothes by grief unkempt,
She told the titans she could not
Betray Sri Ram by word or thought.
His name with Sita did revolve,
As she her life longed to dissolve.

26

Sita in her grief lamented,
And her anguish then was vented:
"Wealth can have no use for me,
Captive in adversity.
A heart of stone does here indwell,
Since my breath would not yet quell.
This body can a meal suffice,
But Ravan cannot me entice.

Separated from my love,
I envy all the gods above,
That they can still observe his face,
While I am captive in this place.
Perhaps he does not pity me,
Since I was carried o'er the sea,
Or laid his weapons down to fast,
As munis have done in the past.
Or now that I am far away,
Does his love no longer stay?
How could my lord desert his love,
Defenseless, like a baby dove?
Assuredly he shall avenge
This insult that did me infringe.
His arrows shall consume this ground
And plumes of smoke will then surround
The wailing widows of these demons,
When they taste the wrath of humans.
Cruel by nature they shall be
Subdued by Ram ferociously.
Perhaps, believing I was killed,
Raghav his own death so willed.
If this is true, I wish to die
And follow him where e'er he lie."

27

The titan women rose in fury,
Threatening to make her curry,
But Trijata told them there,
Not to harm a single hair.
In the night she had a dream,
Their destruction was the theme.
Terrified, those demons asked
To know what in the dream had passed:
"Lakshman, Ram, and Sita came,
Radiant just like a flame,

Upon a car high in the sky,
That on the backs of swans did fly.
Multi-colored garlands graced
Their necks and arms where they were placed,
And brilliant robes of many hues
Draped their bodies and their shoes.
Upon great elephants they rode
And to the sun and moon they strode.
Ravan on the earth there lay,
His clothes of red the ground did splay,
With shaven head and drinking wine,
Laughing on the ground supine.
A woman dragged him here and there,
To the south she did him bear.
Headlong to the earth he fell,
Stinking like the pits of hell.
With a noose around his neck,
And oleander did him deck.
Kumbhakarn and Ravan's son,
From their deaths they tried to run.
Only Bibhishan remained,
Alone he had the kingdom reigned."
Trijata did advise them all,
To before that goddess fall,
And for forgiveness they should ask,
For the evil of their task.
Raghav's victory is near,
To rescue her who is so dear.
All the omens did portend
Attainment of Prince Raghav's end.
Sita, out of true delight,
Knowing of her husband's might,
Said she would give them protection,
Such was Sita's benediction.

28

Separated from her lord,
The well of grief she could not ford,
And finally the threats wore down,
As Sita did in sorrow drown.
And with the cord that tied her hair,
Submerged in waves of deep despair,
Vaidehi did prepare to hang
To end this life of cruel harangue.

29

Then nature gave a wisp of hope
Whereby Vaidehi could now cope.
Twitches down her left side ran,
Predicting victory for man.
Felicity she felt inside,
When knowing Ram to there did ride.

30

Atop the tree that banar sat,
Like a small elusive cat,
And all that passed on down below,
Made him feel Vaidehi's woe.
Still the night did slip away,
And he did not her fears allay.
So quietly the banar thought,
How conversation could be brought.
Still the demons did surround
Vaidehi on the barren ground.
He dared not excite their wrath
When still he had to cross this path.
And how will she believe in him,
When it could be a trick or whim?
But if he could not to her speak,
Her fortitude might grow too weak.

31

As he did review the matter,
Praise of Ram did sweetly chatter:
"Long ago a mighty king,
Who honor to his house did bring,
Acquired a son of peerless might
Who easily his foes could smite.
The father did command his son
The kingdom he would have to shun,
And in the forest would he dwell,
He whose sire did him expel.
His brother and his youthful bride
Ever lingered at his side.
Many were the beasts he slew,
And demons did that one pursue.
His consort by them borne away,
Cast him under sorrow's sway.
While searching for his missing wife
He made a friend throughout his life,
Who gave him all the banar host
To search for her at every post.
I am one who came from there,
Searching for the one so fair,
Able to assume new form,
As anything I can transform."
Then Vaidehi quickly searched
To find where Hanuman was perched.

32

Sita gasped in great surprise
When his form she did apprise:
His face had been severely scarred;
In battle it had been so marred.
Startled by that awesome sight,
Recoiling from the sudden fright,
A banar does misfortune bring,

Lamenting, she born of a king,
Thought it was a frightful dream,
Afraid of what it then could deem.

33

Hanuman slid down the tree,
And approached her carefully.
With joined palms he softly spoke
To she who did his faith evoke.
He did ask who she could be,
Alone and dressed so plaintively.
Through the dust her glory shone,
Her beauty did her dress atone,
She said King Janak was her sire,
He who was devoid of ire.
She was Raghav's wedded wife,
Happily they spent their life.
But he was exiled to the wood,
Yet with him she always stood.
By Ravan she was borne away,
Across the ocean did she stay.
Two months she had left to live,
Until the demons death did give.

34

Like nectar dripping on the heart,
The news of Ram did he impart;
But Sita thought he was the same
As he who changed his form and name.
On the ground she sat exhausted
Thinking she had been accosted.
But her heart was glad to hear
The news about her one so dear.
She thought she did imagine then,
That banar with the coral skin.
But Hanuman to her recounted

How the ocean he surmounted.
Like a messenger was he,
To save her from adversity.

35

In relief did Sita ask
Of Hanuman, to tell his task,
And tell her how this friendship grew
Between the men and banars, too.
News of Ram she longed to hear
And held within her heart so dear.
Everything he told to her,
Each event that did occur:
How the two great friends did meet,
And how King Bāli met defeat,
And how he came to be there now
When all the banars took a vow
To fast to death before the sea,
Failing to find Maithili.
He told her of Ram's burning grief
And how he could find no relief;
Torn by separation, he
Was cast adrift in misery.

36

Hanuman did her assure
That soon her anguish Ram would cure.
He was Raghav's messenger,
As well as Ravan's challenger.
The ring which Ram did give to him,
With his name upon the rim,
He gave to Raghav's blessed wife
And so it did revive her life.
Delightedly she held the ring,
And floods of joy her tears did bring.
And to that dweller of the trees,

She said these words that did him please:
"Oh banar that the trees have teased,
With thee I am most sweetly pleased.
Thy valor does surpass the rest;
Of banars, thou art truly blest.
But tell me how it comes to be,
That Ram does not search here for me?
Why his wrath has not reproached
The ocean or has Lanka broached?
Why this awful quietude,
When I by Ravan was subdued?
Could it be he does not grieve,
Or my peril not perceive?
Will he not deliver me,
Far from him, in misery?
Bharat does not send a force
To Raghav's army reinforce?
Will Sugriva send his host
Of banars to this fearful post?
Where is Lakshman and his shaft,
To display his martial craft?
Will Raghav meet with victory,
And rescue me from agony?
Has his luster dimmed from grief?
Is he firm in his belief?
I only live to hear his name,
To hear of Ram, I do remain."
With these words Vaidehi waited,
News of Ram made her elated.
Hanuman to her replied
These words that did her love confide:
"Raghav knows not where you are;
None from you can now him bar.
His sorrow makes the earth to steam,
In sympathy the rivers stream.
Sleep abandoned him and left

Since of you he was bereft.
Every small frivolity
Reminds him of his tragedy.
Your jewels unto his breast he clasped,
As he sobbed and weakly gasped.
The flies and worms torment his lot,
But for his body he cares not.
When he learns where you've been found
His forces will this fort surround."
Like shadows passing on the moon,
Her face became an ancient rune,
With joy hearing of her lord,
And sorrow at the grief untoward.

37

Every creature has its fate,
The time of which, none can abate.
After Ravan has been slain,
Sita shall her consort gain.
Counsellors of Ravan told
That monarch that he was too bold,
And Vaidehi should return
To Ram, before his wrath did burn.
But wise words are not received
By those who are by fate deceived.
Raghav with his banar host
Would defeat this demon post.
She could climb and fly upon
The mighty back of Hanuman.
Across the sea and reach to Ram,
Felicity to gain therefrom.
But Maithili of him did ask,
How he could fulfil this task,
When such a tiny banar he,
Could he leap across the sea?
Then Hanuman, his form revealed,

A mammoth size he so did yield.
His prowess to her did he claim,
That all the worlds knew of his fame.
With wisdom, beauty, and with taste,
Vaidehi said these words so chaste:
"Your prowess that you do reveal,
To my heart it does appeal.
With thee I know I could return
To see the one for whom I yearn,
But would I not fall in the sea,
By the wind's velocity?
Or if they should a battle seek,
My hold on thee would be too weak.
On this journey I could die,
As we across the ocean fly.
For chastity, I dare not touch
Another's body, e're so much.
And if you did return me there,
Raghav's fame it would impair.
Ram can slay this boundless host,
Of his strength I do not boast.
With Lakshman ever at his side,
Nowhere can these demons hide."

38

Of her speech he had approved,
And by her modesty was moved.
The words that Hanuman had spoken,
Of his love did prove a token.
Then of Sita did he ask,
A message to complete his task.
With broken words between each sob,
She spoke of love that time does rob:
"Oh my love across the sea,
We used to dwell so pleasantly,
By the vast Mandakini

In groves adorned so graciously.
On my breast you laid your head
To rest upon a fragrant bed,
After sporting in the lake,
Your thirst with water did you slake.
A crow as black as sable night
Arose, intent with me to fight.
I threw a stone but it remained
Convinced that I should now be tamed.
My girdle did I throw at him,
And so my robe fell to my hem.
You laughed and then I blushed in shame,
And then into your arms I came.
You pacified my childish fear,
And held me to you very near.
On thy breast I went to sleep
And you, in turn, on mine did keep.
When I arose it did attack
While you slept upon your back.
He tore my breast and blood did seep,
And instantly you woke from sleep.
That crow, who was Devendra's son,
Stood aloof, an evil one.
By the time that you could blink,
Into the earth, that crow did sink.
With a blade of kusha grass,
Your mantra on the blade did pass,
And bursting into golden flame,
Upon that crow your shaft did aim.
He had through the regions passed,
Seeking you, he came at last.
Mercy did he seek from thee,
And thou did grant it willingly.
The shaft could not be loosed in vain,
And so its right eye did obtain.
How is it that you fail me now,

When I am like a tethered cow?"
But Hanuman did faith evince,
And said they would be coming hence.
He asked to know what should he say,
What words of hers he could convey.
"On my behalf, you should inquire,
The welfare of those sons of fire.
Of Sugriva, do beseech,
With kind and measured fruitful speech,
To rescue me without delay,
My hopes upon them all do lay.
When two months have passed away
Ravan surely will me slay."
Then as Vaidehi softly wept,
She took a pearl, in secret kept,
And gave it to the Son of Wind,
And to Prince Raghav did it send.

39

That pearl she wore upon her brow,
Which she gave that banar now,
To the mind of Ram would bring
Memories, a faded king.
She bade that banar to convey
To them all not to delay,
And happiness she wished for all;
Their memories she did recall.
Hanuman to her predicted
Ravan soon would be evicted.
Hanuman did solace bring,
As if he were a breath of spring.
She asked that banar yet to wait
Another day, if not too late.
Her life as yet remained in peril,
Hanuman could not be idle.
So that banar reassured

Vaidehi, still by dust obscured,
The bhalukas and banars there,
Soon would free her of all care.
Reunited she would be,
Released from all uncertainty.

40

Sita to that one confided,
That her life in Ram abided.
After one more month had passed,
She would yield her life at last.
But now that Hanuman had found
That beauty through the worlds renowned,
Her misery would soon be ended,
She on all of them depended.
Blessings she did then bestow,
As Hanuman in size did grow.

41

With respect he took his leave,
Now his mission to achieve.
Yet still he did reflect within,
How he could a battle win,
And assess their strength and pride,
And then the news to Ram confide.
The grove where all the consorts went,
Soon by Hanuman was rent.
Everything of beauty laid,
Now a pile of trash he made.
He broke the trees and ripped the creeper,
Standing like the garden keeper,
Waiting for them to appear,
Brandishing their sword and spear.

42

The uproar of his ravaging
Sent the titans scavenging.
The titan women Sita asked,
Who this banar was unmasked.
She told them all she did not know
That banar who had laid it low.
They hurried back to Ravan's court;
The matter to him, did report.
In anger both his eyes did flash
And scaldingly did orders lash.
Who would dare to talk to her,
The one that Ravan did deter?
Eighty thousand titans ran
To fight that angry banar man.
With mace and hook and sword and spear,
They came to him who had no fear.
Like a mountain did he stand,
Alone he fought and bare of hand.
To them did he loudly roar,
He crossed the sea onto their shore.
A messenger of Ram was he,
And he would crush them easily.
Lanka would he now destroy,
He who was Sri Ram's envoy.
Demons did assail that one
But quickly was the battle won
As Hanuman flew through the air
A rod of iron he then did bare.
When Ravan heard his host was slain,
He sent another one in vain.

43

The temple standing on the mountain
Flowing with sweet water fountain,
Was by Hanuman destroyed

As the guards with spears deployed.
They were quickly by him slain,
They could not that one constrain.
Hanuman stood in the air
Roaring like a mountain there.
"Victory to Ram I vow,
Lakshman, I will show you how!
Millions more come forth like me
To lead the way to victory!"

44

Ravan sent Prahasta's son
To fight with that voracious one.
His chariot was drawn by asses,
Wearing great vermillion sashes.
Letting loose his bow to twang,
The mountain with its echo rang.
On Hanuman his arrows flew
But they could not that one subdue.
Hanuman did seize a boulder,
Raising it upon his shoulder,
Threw it at that demon's car,
Who scattered it with shafts afar.
Hanuman tore up a tree
And whirled it most ferociously,
But Jambumali ran it through,
And Hanuman was wounded, too.
His body by those shafts was covered,
While he in the air had hovered.
In a rage that banar rushed,
Hurled a club, the demon crushed.
Jambumali, overcome,
Then to death he did succumb.
The sons of Ravan's minister,
Voracious and quite sinister,

Prepared with Hanuman to fight,
Like moths into a searing light.

45

Seven titans followed course,
With a full battalion force,
Where that banar at the gate
Eagerly did them await.
They poured their arrows from the sky;
That banar did around them fly.
And with his arms and chest he smote
Those warriors while death did gloat.
The army ran in each direction
Seeking where it could, protection.

46

Ravan did conceal his fears,
As he did approach his peers.
His generals he did address
With strategies that did impress.
All precautions they should take,
Their thirst for blood, on him would slake.
Like the rising sun so bright,
Hanuman was primed to fight.
Their shafts at him were soon discharged
As Hanuman his form enlarged.
His roaring shook the firmament
As he did the army rent.
Three generals soon met their death,
And Hanuman, not out of breath,
Withstood their axes and their spear,
He who had no trace of fear,
And tearing off the mountain top,
Those demons did he swiftly stop.
Then at the gate he paused to rest
Waiting for the next to test.

47

When Ravan learned his men were slain,
Anger did his ire sustain.
His youthful son was Aksha named,
For skill and valor he was famed.
His celestial car ascended,
Swift as thought his horses wended,
Beautiful, adorned in gold,
The chariot was lightning bold.
To Hanuman he quickly rode,
His fierce glance did courage bode.
And with the spirit of a lion,
He attacked that beast of iron.
There a fight between them waged
That none before had ever gauged.
And the sun and wind grew still,
For fear their battle did instill.
The waters in the ocean churned
And fearfully the earth had turned.
Happily, this banar fought
That warrior whom fame had sought.
Hanuman in exultation,
For his foe had great laudation.
Many were the shafts he threw,
As Hanuman between them flew.
Pierced by that marksman's aim,
His roar upon the heavens came.
With great skill beyond his years,
Aksha did excel his peers.
His prowess one cannot ignore,
In battle it increases more.
Though Hanuman was loath to slay
This hero, yet he would him stay.
His chariot the banar smashed;
By his palm his car was trashed.
But Aksha in the air arose,

Ascending to Lord Yama's throes,
As Hanuman did grab his feet
And spun him like an earthen skeet.
Hanuman upon him tread
As Aksha on the ground lay dead.
A chilling icicle of fear,
Ravan's heart did catch and spear.

48

Ravan called his eldest son,
Indrajit, whom wars had won,
Experienced in martial art;
He alone could fill the part.
His car was drawn by lions, four,
That swiftly through the heavens soar.
His car did rumble like a storm,
The thunder quickly did inform
The corners of the world that he
Was 'gaging in hostility.
Hanuman enlarged his shape,
The splendor of the sun did scrape.
Darkening the firmament,
As shrieks and howls, the heavens rent.
Together they engaged in battle
And the sound caused earth to rattle.
Hanuman, his shafts eluded,
By a dance he executed.
Agile through the friendly air,
His graceful moves beyond compare,
Indrajit could not him catch,
Angrily, his thoughts did hatch.
A boon of Brahma he recalled,
A weapon that its foes enthralled.
Hanuman by it was bound;
Brahma's rope around him wound.
To honor what the Lord had sired,

Hanuman the fight retired.
Recognizing Brahma's will,
He upon the ground was still.
Hanuman they quickly bound,
A rope around him then was wound.
The spell of Brahma was annulled.
By the binding it was nulled.
They thought they had the upper hand
But that is what the banar planned.
And Hanuman allowed it so,
His hidden purpose did not show.
And so they dragged him to the court,
As if a monkey they did sport.
The ministers did of him ask
Who he was, and what his task.
He said he was Sugriva's aide,
And fought with them as he was bade.
Hanuman is how they know
This banar who defeats his foe.

49

Hanuman beheld that king
Who filled him with great wondering.
His massive form was like a cloud
Of purple hue with mist enshroud.
From within that thunder-hold,
A light illumined, like to gold.
With bracelets on his arms and rings,
He was the king of all the kings.
Infinite, his might and strength,
None could measure it in length.
His concentrated mind was coarse;
It was the source of all his force.
If he had a righteous hand,
He could have ruled the skies and land.

50

Before the court that banar stood
And all their insults he withstood.
They wished to know from where he came,
The reason and his truthful name.
To their questions he replied,
Before them he had testified.
Prince Raghav was his allied friend;
He came to expedite his end.
He was as he appeared to be,
A banar in reality.
A boon from God he did receive,
That his life-breaths would not leave,
He could choose when he would die,
On his will it did rely.

51

Hanuman, both strong and wise,
The situation did surmise,
And offered Ravan good advice
To save that land of lust and vice:
"For Sugriva I have come;
He does not to fear succumb.
His counsel is both wise and true;
Justice does that one pursue.
The House of Raghu had a king
And with him righteousness did bring.
Dasharatha ruled his land
With a kind and gentle hand.
Ram and Lakshman are his sons,
Effulgent like two rising suns.
The injunction of his sire
Sent Prince Raghav to retire,
With his brother and his wife
To lead a simple austere life.
In the forest they did live,

Protection to the saints did give.
In Janasthan, that savage wood,
Sita, Ram and Lakshman stood.
One fateful day she disappeared,
Sita, whom her lord revered.
Out of love for Maithili,
Raghav searched relentlessly.
As he looked, a friend was found;
Sugriva and Sri Ram are bound.
Bāli by Prince Ram was slain;
The throne did Prince Sugriva gain.
Now the banars scour the earth
In search for her of pious birth.
Born of wind, I am his son,
Known to all as Hanuman.
Four hundred miles across the sea
I travelled to find Maithili.
The law of dharma you have crossed,
Righteousness from you is lost.
To Ram you should return his wife
Or Sri Ram will end your life.
None among the worlds can stand
The wrath loosed from Prince Raghav's hand.
You invited death to you
When Sita you chose to pursue.
Though you did receive the boon
From death by some you are immune;
But man and banar can ensnare
You into Lord Yama's lair.
The whole of Lanka I could cleave
If the mandate I receive.
The power of Sri Ram can make
The earth to crumble or to quake.
None can vanquish him, it's true,
The one who does his mind subdue."
When Ravan heard this fruitful word

The wrath within him churned and stirred.
The death of Hanuman he urged,
As his anger through him surged.

52

Bibhishan did him appease
With words that did the monarch please.
A messenger does not death meet,
He does another's will entreat.
Punishments can then be given
As he is so homeward driven.
He should seek the one who sent
The messenger with his consent.

53

Ravan did his words concede,
And thought what punishment to cede.
To burn his tail and then parade
That banar through the town's arcade,
Is the punishment they'd mete,
As if they could enforce this feat.
Hanuman in ropes was bound,
And his tail with rags was wound.
But he then enlarged his form,
As the demons 'round did swarm.
But they could not that one perturb,
As they led him down the curb.
Then his tail was set ablaze,
This his balance could not faze.
The titans did so laugh and taunt,
But Hanuman they could not daunt.
The news to Sita was relayed,
That her friend in ropes was stayed.
Sita did beseech the fire
To satisfy her deep desire,
And not to burn a single hair

Of that Ranger of the Air.
The fire was cool upon his tail,
As Sita's prayer did then prevail.
And Hanuman did break the rope,
And from the gate did Lanka scope.

54

From house to house that banar leapt,
And all of them by fire were swept.
The titan women shrieked and cried,
As they were stripped of all their pride.
Jewels and metals made an ore
That from their palaces did pour.
Lanka was a conflagration,
Devas cried in jubilation.
Hanuman apart could see,
Lanka blazing fiercely.
Like the God of Fire he stood,
None of them his ire withstood.
Then he bounded to the sea
And put his tail there soothingly.

55

Suddenly that banar felt
A wave of dread upon his pelt,
As he remembered Janaki,
Alone in this perversity.
Anger marred his clarity
As he forgot all charity,
And torched the city by his ire,
Everything was set afire:
"Verily one's wrath consumes
A man of reason when it fumes.
Every cruel perversity,
In all its vast diversity,
Can cause a righteous man to act

Like an evil one in fact;
Anger easily can sway
A man and cast his sense away.
What heinous sin did I commit
When Janaki I did forget,
And cast the city into flame?
Her death on me alone can blame.
My master's aim has been defeated,
When by fire she was mistreated.
I will end my life today;
But none this sin can cast away.
Or could it be the fire protected
She who is by all respected?
Certainly she can consume
The fire alone with every fume.
But how can fire this devi touch,
When her love for Ram is such?"

56

Hanuman approached the wife
Of Ram, who had retained her life.
And he bowed to take his leave
From her, though still her heart did grieve.
Her eyes did gaze upon him long
As if they heard a distant song.
Could that army cross the sea,
Full of death and treachery?
Hanuman she did beseech,
To tell them quickly to here reach.
Ram, his prowess could so show
By vanquishing his mortal foe.
Hanuman spoke words at length
So Sita could regain her strength:
Soon Kakutstha would be there;
Yield not to her deep despair.
Hanuman resolved to cross

The sea and all its floating dross.
The highest mountain he ascended
Bounding through the trees he fended.
Thirty miles into the sky
That mountain with its peaks did lie.
Forty miles across the land
That mountain had the island spanned.
When Hanuman prepared to leap
It was reduced into a heap,
And that which once rose in the air
Was leveled to the ground right there.
High into the air he bounded,
All the beings were astounded.

57

Above the sea and through the cloud,
Hanuman in might was proud.
As he pushed the clouds aside,
And on the tail of wind did ride,
Hanuman did blaze above,
Remembering Prince Raghav's love.
He wagged his tail and gave a roar,
As thunder heard upon the shore,
And there his friends did him await,
Wondering what was his fate.
In victory that banar growled,
As through the air he lightly prowled,
And on the shore he came to land,
As once again, the sea he spanned.
His friends around him roared and cheered,
Relieved that he had reappeared.
And from his lips that banar cried
That he had seen Prince Raghav's bride.

58

As their eyes on him did gaze,
And they all were filled with praise,
Eagerly they did await,
His adventures to relate.
And Hanuman did then reveal
Everything of his ordeal.
All the stories were recounted,
How his obstacles surmounted.

59

Now he asked them to decide
What action would some good betide.
Janaki did there grow frail;
Their mission now should not her fail.
Faithful to her wedded spouse,
Her purity he did espouse.

60

Angada to them suggested
Sita should by them be wrested
From the peril Ravan planned,
And they would raze his home and land.
Ravan would they quickly vanquish,
Putting forth an end to anguish.
Janaki they would return
To Ram, who still for her did yearn.
Jambavan dismissed their schemes
For Ram should rescue her, it seems.
The mandate was for them to find
The one who lives within his mind.
From her peril to deliver
To Sri Ram, the earth's lawgiver.

61

Joyfully, they had no care,
As they leapt high in the air.
Victorious they would return,
And pride in each of them did burn.
The garden known as Madhuvan,
Soon they all did bound upon.
Fragrant with celestial trees
They longed to pause and take their ease.
Angada permission gave
In honor of their deeds so brave.
They ate the honey in the trees,
Swarming with petulant bees.
Every fruit they did there taste,
In doing so, the trees did waste.
Soon they were inebriated
As they freely celebrated.
Dadhimukha was its guard,
Protecting that celestial yard.
He the banars disregarded,
Though he was by them vanguarded.
Words turned into slaps and blow,
And Dadhimukha they laid low.

62

The garden grove they soon did ravish,
Imitating piles of rubbish.
Gleefully they smote the guard
Between their knees they pressed them hard.
Inebriated by the drink,
They lost capacity to think.
Ululating very loud,
Of their prowess they were proud.
Dadhimukha they did crush;
To Sugriva did he rush.

63

Prostrate at his feet he lay,
And of the news he did convey
That Madhuvan had they laid waste,
That garden which had long been chaste.
Angada and every friend,
The honey and the fruits did vend.
And all the guards they did confuse
As they tried to stop their ruse.
Sugriva did rejoice at heart,
Not begrudging them their part.
In victory one can behave
Like a child or foolish knave.
He requested him to bring
Those banars to their sovereign king.
To Ram and Lakshman he informed,
The banars had the garden stormed,
Indicating great success,
An end to their ordeal and stress.

64

Dadhimukha had returned
Unto the ones he just had spurned.
In pleasant words he then conveyed
The order which on him was laid.
In unison did they rejoice,
Praising him in single voice.
In the air they all did bound,
Emitting such an awesome sound,
As they cried in victory
Exulting in their revelry.
Sugriva then his friends consoled,
That their actions had foretold
That Janaki by them was found,
Their cries did through the air resound.
That banar host before them bowed,

Accomplishing what they had vowed,
And Hanuman pronounced that word,
Which joy in their hearts then stirred:
"Sita has been seen by me,"
Whereby they felt felicity.

65

Hanuman to Ram recounted
How the grief in Sita mounted.
Day by day she wastes away,
But her love does never stray.
Ever fixed in thought on Ram,
So her days and nights pass from.
After one more month has passed,
She vowed to end her life at last.
Ten months had she been abducted
And her love for Ram obstructed.
Sita's message for her lord,
Hanuman to him restored.
The pearl that Sita did bestow,
Ram received with hope and woe.

66

Tears from Ram and Lakshman flowed,
The sorrow on their faces showed.
The pearl unto his heart he clasped,
And then of Hanuman he asked
To tell him more, to speak to them
The words that she had meant for him.
King Janak had acquired that gem
From Indra, who was pleased with him.
She wore it on their wedding day,
Deep within, its light did play.
Her beauty by it was enhanced,
And Ram by her was thus entranced.

67-68

Everything he did repeat,
Not a word he would delete.
Every detail was relayed
That Hanuman to Ram conveyed.
Every gesture, every sigh,
Every move and every cry,
All details he did relate,
But still Ram's grief did not abate.

Yuddha Kāṇḍa

YUDDHA KĀṆḌA is the description of the war between Rama and Ravana. The banar army marches to the sea shore. At Lanka, the demons persuade Ravana to make war. Ravana's younger brother, Bibhishan, advises Ravana to return Sita to Rama and make peace. Ravana threatens him, so Bibhishan leaves Lanka to seek protection with Rama. The divine architect Vishwakarma constructs a bridge across the sea to help Rama and the banar army reach Lanka. The banars and demons engage in battle. Many fierce battles take place. Indrajit, the son of Ravana, is slain by Lakshman. Ravana's battle with Rama lasts for many days. Finally, Ravana is slain by Rama. Bibhishan is installed as King of Lanka. Rama sends for Sita; then renounces her because she was captive in another man's house for so long. Sita enters the fire to prove her chastity and the God of Fire and the devas attest to her purity. They all ascend the divine chariot pushpak and return to Ayodhya. Rama is installed as King of Ayodhya.

Yuddha Kāṇḍa

1

Like sun upon the banks of snow,
Raghav's heart was set aglow.
Ram embraced his noble friend,
His boundless love could find no end.
In salutary words he spoke,
The feelings that it did evoke:
"In the hour of my need,
You rescued me in thought and deed.
Your courage and your valor, too,
All of Lanka did subdue.
Yet when I have the sea perceived,
By misery I am deceived.
Anxiety does me beset,
How the mission can be met."
Silently Prince Raghav thought,
How the end could now be sought.

2

Sugriva in this vein consoled
Sri Ram with words both wise and bold:
"Fear upon the mind subdues
A man who victory pursues.
Impotence is the result

When fear your mind does once consult.
Success is gained by he who knows
His Self, then all his sorrow goes.
This field of banars is arrayed
With weapons to the foe abrade.
Concert thy energies to build
A bridge, that is by thee self-willed.
The banars shall cross o'er the sea,
Confident of victory.
One who is both swift and strong,
Conquers and in life is long.
Thy princess does await for thee,
And thou shalt win with dignity.
All the omens do portend,
Ravan, we shall apprehend."

3

Ram addressed that valiant one,
Known to all as Hanuman,
To describe that citadel,
Lanka, where the demons dwell.
"Elephants do guard the gate,
And piles of spears do them await,
At four impressive, massive doors,
Enforced with iron and precious ores.
Chariots and catapult,
Are ready to withstand assault.
Pearls and gems adorn a wall,
Standing like a mountain tall.
The city is by it encased,
Impossible to scale in haste.
Icy waters do surround
The wall where crocodiles abound.
Cannons do defend their bridges,
Seasoned with sharp spiky ridges.
Ravan ever waits to fight—

That deadly Ranger of the Night.
Strong and cruel, the king is bold,
And Lanka lies within his hold.
Impregnable, this citadel,
Where the king within does dwell.
Atop a barren rock resides,
The boundless ocean at its sides.
Countless demons there defend
That citadel in every bend.
I tore their walls and filled the moat,
The ramparts and the land I smote.
Let us pass that vast expanse
Of sea, and on their heads will dance."

4

At the time when planets passed,
With stars and moon in favor, cast,
The orders issued now to wend
Their journey to the southern end.
The general did scout the way,
Alert for any hidden fray,
Where the fruits and roots abound,
And water could by them be found.
On Hanuman Sri Ram did ride
With Lakshman ever at his side.
On Angada Prince Lakshman rode,
And all the banars bravely strode.
They jumped and ran and leapt around,
In all directions they did bound.
The trees and shrubs they brandished there,
Each the other's strength did dare,
And their flanks did highly guard,
With Nila as their troop's vanguard.
Lakshman to his brother spoke,
In words that confidence evoke,
That all auspicious signs were there,

And victory would be their fare.
Swiftly as the wind they ran,
As they passed across this span,
And a cloud of dust did rise,
Covering the sun and skies.
They did not pause or even rest,
So anxious to their strength attest.
They crossed the scented mountain range,
And fruits and roots they did exchange.
Mahendra mountain they did climb
Whose beauty was to all sublime.
They camped upon the southern shore
And paused to think what furthermore.
The sun did set and moon did rise,
Tranquility belied their eyes.
The endless waves rolled on the shore,
Yet the sea increased no more.
Fathomless the ocean lay,
And gentle mist on them did spray.
The image of the moon did trace
Across the water's silent face.
Boundless did the ocean seem,
Like a meadow veiled in dream.

5

Ram to Lakshman softly spoke
The feelings that it did evoke:
"Oh gentle breeze upon the wind,
Swiftly to my consort wend,
And softly through her tresses blow,
Whispering her name so low.
Then return to me so fast,
That I can smell her scent at last,
And know that what has touched her hair,
To me, has wafted through the air.
When shall my eyes her form behold,

She who's radiant like gold?
When shall I feel her gentle touch
She whom I do love so much?
The gentle hour of her youth,
Is cast in shadow like a sleuth.
Frail by nature she becomes
Thinner and to grief succumbs.
An ageless love binds her with me,
A love born from eternity."

6

After Hanuman had left,
And Lanka had by him been cleft,
Ravan did consult his aide,
Their course of action to be laid,
He sought the elder's wise advice
What action would their end suffice.
To deliberate the question,
He was open to suggestion.

7

The titans told him not to fear,
For they were his with sword and spear.
Yaksha, dānava, and titan,
Easily could Ravan frighten.
He subdued the serpent race
When he descended to their place.
Even Indra was defeated,
By his son he was depleted.
Indrajit should Ravan send
To vanquish Ram, his life to end.

8

Intoxicated with their pride
His generals did Ram deride.
Each the other did outboast,

Trying to impress their host.
Single-handedly they claimed,
That banar by them would be maimed.
Alone they could defeat the host
Of banars ranging coast to coast.
And what to say of human men?
Soon the battle they would win.
And so they did advise their king,
That victory each one could bring.

9

The one whose senses are controlled,
And the Lord does him uphold,
Is not so easy to defeat,
The titans praise their own conceit.
Bibhishan advised the king
Destruction to his home did bring,
By harboring Vaidehi there.
When her to Ram they should repair.
Ravan to his room retired,
To contemplate on what transpired.

10

The dawn upon the day did break,
As all within the fort did wake,
And Bibhishan then did proceed,
To utter words for all to heed.
Ravan in his chamber seated,
Bibhishan in silence greeted.
Aided by his minister,
Ravan was quite sinister.
Bibhishan expressed his doubt,
Hoping to bring him about:
"Since Janaki has here been brought,
The heart of Lanka has been caught,
And evil omens here portend

The maladjustment of your end.
The sacrificial fire does choke
And offerings are veiled in smoke.
Snakes and ants do here abide,
In offerings they now reside;
The kine are dry and horses neigh,
Asses cry and ichors stay.
Crows do swarm above our head
And vultures circle for the dead.
Beasts approach our gates at night,
And growl and fight until the light.
All within the court agree,
The cause of this does lie with thee.
Return Vaidehi free from harm,
And quickly do this war disarm."
Ravan would not hear or heed,
He was lost to lust and greed.

11

On Sita, Ravan always dwelled,
As pride and lust within him swelled.
Through the streets that titan rode,
As if he did his subjects goad.
He was flanked on every side
By his guards as he did ride.
He went to the assembly hall,
And all the titans there, did call.
Trumpeters the king did herald,
He whose prowess was unrivaled.
Vishvakarma did construct
This hall for meetings to conduct.
A floor of gold and throne of pearl,
And banners that they did unfurl,
Adorned that spacious convocation
At this most severe occasion.

All within the hall grew still,
Silence did the spaces fill.

12

Ravan, full of arrogance,
Throughout the titans cast his glance:
"The army does surround the gate,
For instructions do they wait.
Kumbhakarn from sleep arose;
Retaliation now we pose.
What course of action should we take?
Our reputation is at stake.
Since my eyes on Sita fell,
My thoughts upon her always dwell.
Goaded by intense desire,
I am consumed by passion's fire.
We will not return the wife
Of Ram, but take his mortal life.
How can banars cross the sea?
Surely ours is victory!"
Kumbhakarn did wave his arm
And filled the hall with great alarm:
"To take another's wife by force
Has led thee down a heedless course.
Your elders you did not consult,
And now there is a grave result.
To go against established law,
Is in thee a doubtful flaw.
But I will kill these men for thee,
And lead thee to quick victory.
The banar host I shall consume,
In me, they have addressed their doom."

13

The general did ask the king,
Why he did Vaidehi bring,

And not enjoy her as he will,
And take from her his ample fill.
But long ago occurred a scene
Where Ravan acted quite obscene:
To worship Brahma she did go,
Her beauty through the clouds did glow.
This nymph was coursing through the sky
When Ravan did that one espy.
Soon deflowered by that one,
Thus she was by fate undone.
She approached the heaven's sire,
And told Him what did there transpire.
On Ravan, Brahma laid a curse,
That if he does a girl coerce
Against her will to take his bed,
The Lord will shatter Ravan's head.
That is why he cannot force
Vaidehi to adopt his course.
But Ravan is deceived by pride—
Thinks nothing of Prince Raghav's side.

14

All were vainful of their strength,
Convinced to go to any length,
Confident they would defeat
Raghav, who could not compete.
But Bibhishan did warn again
That none could beat the Best of Men.
None his prowess could withstand,
In spite of what the king had planned.
Vaidehi was a noose disguised,
And Bibhishan again advised,
Vaidehi should they now return
To Ram, before his wrath does burn.

15

Incensed by Bibhishan's good sense,
Indrajit did him dispense:
"Oh youngest brother of my sire,
Fear and cowardice conspire
Within thy breast, to speak this word,
Have you not of Ravan heard?
Indra was by me cast out,
Renounce your fear and childish doubt.
These mortal men I can defeat,
For me it is a simple feat."
Bibhishan to him replied,
In truth which angered all their pride:
"Childish words from you I hear,
Conducive to our woe, I fear.
Still unripe upon the vine,
The song of death I hear you whine.
A son you do appear to be,
But death you are in certainty.
The wrath of Ram dries up the sea,
This is the truth I speak to thee.
With ornaments, celestial gem,
We should return his wife to him."

16

By this speech he gave affront,
So Ravan then did him confront:
"A foe parading as a friend
Can lead us to destruction's end.
The relatives of one resent
The fortune that another's lent.
Self-interested you seem to be,
As we have been used by thee.
A curse be laid upon thy head,
Another would have long been dead!"
Insulted, Bibhishan arose,

He, where dharma does repose:
"To spare thee from the noose of death,
The truth I uttered with my breath.
But he who has no self-control,
Virtue cannot him extol.
Death through Sita now does woo,
But in the end you'll Sita rue.
I take my leave and wish thee well,
For Sita is the cloak of hell."
So in the air that titan stood
And four with him who understood.

17

In the blinking of an eye,
Bibhishan from there did fly,
Arriving at the southern coast
Where Sugriva had his host.
Sugriva and his men did bare
Their weapons, to them in the air.
Convinced that they had come to fight,
The banars did reveal their might.
Bibhishan, with mind controlled
With his friends of courage bold,
Addressed Sugriva standing there,
That they did not for war prepare:
"I stand before you to attest
That Ravan did Ram's consort wrest,
And he has cast me from his land
Because I doubted what he planned.
He would not regard advice,
Addicted to his lust and vice,
So I have sought Prince Raghav's feet,
Protection there I do entreat.
His younger brother I am known,
As Bibhishan to you am shown.
Please inform your Lord and king,

That Bibhishan his aid does bring."
Ram and Lakshman were informed
By Sugriva, who forewarned
That Bibhishan had come to sow
Dissension in their ranks and row.
An emissary of their foe,
His intentions did not show.
Ram desired each one to say
How they should this matter play.
Though the truth to Ram was known,
His deference to them was shown.
They all agreed that this did call
For caution on the parts of all.
Interrogation should proceed,
And then they could assess the need.
One who issues from the foe,
They should slowly get to know.
He was not to them a knave,
By the speech or form he gave.
To Ram his nature was revealed,
No motive was therein concealed,
Unless it was to rule his land,
For that he needed Raghav's hand.

18

For one who seeks the lotus feet
Of Ram, there refuge will he meet.
Friend or foe it matters not,
When Ram's compassion has been sought.
Can one be trusted who betrays
His friend or brother in the frays?
The enemies of kings are two:
Relatives and neighbors who
Turn their backs in times of trial,
For their safety give denial.
Ravan does mistrust his kin,

Peace he never finds within.
Their land he does not covet here
For this they have not any fear.
But still among them doubt prevailed,
Treachery is what they hailed.
But Ram for this was not concerned,
His motive he had thus discerned.
For Ram there was no mortal danger
Not from yaksha or night ranger.
Shelter cannot be denied
To one who seeks it at your side.

19

Bibhishan stood on the ground,
Now he had Prince Raghav found.
Everything he left behind,
In hopes he could there refuge find.
He bowed before his lotus feet,
His love for Ram within was sweet.
Ram intently gazed at him,
To understand his mind and whim.
Of Bibhishan, he asked to know;
The weakness of his mortal foe.
Bibhishan to him replied,
Truthfully, he did confide:
"No immortal can him harm,
Ravan causes all alarm.
Kumbhakarn, immense in might,
Sleeps for months within one night.
Indrajit secured the arts
Of magic and celestial darts.
Voracious titans death do scorn,
And scavenge through the dead we mourn.
The gods to Ravan did succumb,
Each that king does overcome."
Raghav to that one assured

That Ravan soon would be abjured,
Then Lanka would receive her king
As Bibhishan, whom Ram would bring.
Then that titan was anointed,
As the king he was appointed.
All the banars hailed and praised,
For Bibhishan in rank was raised.
At the counselors' request,
Bibhishan did then suggest
That Ram, who has the moon-like face,
Should seek assistance from his race.
The ocean would assist the Lord
And banars to its surface ford.
The plan did meet with all their favor,
His advice they all did savor.
So they would approach the sea
To take them to the enemy.

20

A titan spy by Ravan sent,
To the camp of Raghav went.
Returning back unto his king,
With news of them the spy did bring.
Boundless as the vast expanse,
The banar host assumed its stance.
Shuka did that monarch call,
To seek Sugriva and forestall.
The message to that one should bring,
Directly to that banar king,
That Ravan is to him a brother,
Why should they fight one another?
Turn to his ancestral throne,
For Ravan can't be overthrown.
So Shuka rose into the air,
And swiftly met the banars there.
Before he could complete his word,

The banars rose with standing fur,
And as they leapt into the air,
They beat him with their fists right there.
As a messenger he pleaded,
He should not be thus mistreated.
Ram did order them to halt,
And saved him from a grave assault.
Shuka asked the banar king
What words to Ravan he should bring.
To that titan he replied,
This message to his king betide:
"I welcome not these evil brothers
Who desire the death of others.
Lacking pity and compassion,
Death shall be your meted ration.
Nowhere shall you e're escape
The wrath of Ram upon thy nape.
In ignorance you seem to be
Deluded in your majesty."
Then Angada accused that spy,
To count their forces he did try.
That titan should they now arrest,
He was just a spy at best.
The banars bounded in the air
And ruthlessly they seized him there.
Shuka's eyes they tried to pierce,
Banars could be cruel and fierce.
If he died his deeds would fall
Upon Sri Ram, demerits all.
Raghav ordered him released—
Then brutality had ceased.

21

The mighty Ram lay on the shore,
His broadened arms that bracelets bore,
Became his pillow in the sand

As he slept upon his hand.
For three nights on kusha grass,
Raghav did with patience pass.
With gentle words he did appeal,
To Sagara himself reveal.
But after three nights passed this way,
Raghav did no longer pray.
Because of Raghav's mild attempt,
The ocean showed him vile contempt.
Filled with wrath, Ram took his bow
And tremors through the earth did sow.
The arrows in his quiver smoked,
Responding to the wrath provoked.
The ocean waters steamed and churned,
Boiling from his ire that burned.
And Ram released his fiery shaft
That burst in flames as it did waft.
The ocean rose, a monstrous wave,
As serpents tried their lives to save,
And devas in the air cried, "Halt!"
Ram should stop this vain assault.
Lakshman stayed Ram's mighty arm,
To vent his anger caused alarm.

22

Raghav like a menace loomed,
He who was by wrath consumed.
He fixed his shaft upon his bow
And fierce winds began to blow,
Uprooting trees and mountain peak,
As waves upon the shore did streak.
And the sky was cast in shadow,
Like a widow in her sorrow.
Thunder clapped and tremors shook
The earth, like fish upon a hook.
Meteors blazed through the sky,

Unmoved, the shaft with Ram did lie.
Sagara from there arose,
His golden skin with luster glows.
With pearls upon his aqua chest,
The ocean churned upon its breast.
The ocean and the rivers came,
Approaching Ram who was aflame.
The ocean did address that prince
With words that did the truth evince:
"Each element its nature has,
Abiding by the law whereas,
Not by love, desire or fear,
Can its nature change or veer.
But you may cross upon the sea,
The banars may pass easily."
Ram unto the ocean said
This shaft of fire must still be fed.
Where should now this arrow fly?
Once evoked it cannot lie.
"To the north there is a band
Of robbers living on the land.
Daily do they drink from me,
Those denizens of treachery.
To those marauders let it fly,
So they will perish there and die."
The shaft was loosed and fell to there,
And all upon that land turned bare.
The waters of the ocean dried,
A desert there does now abide.
The crater where the arrow fell
Released the waters deep from hell.
But Ramachandra blessed that place,
And now it has a healing grace.
Rich in pasture and in fruits,
Honey-laden, bearing roots,
Free from illness it became;

Throughout the worlds it gathered fame.
"The son of Vishvakarma stands
With power in his nimble hands.
Nala is that deva's son,
The bridge by him is quickly done.
Upon my waters it will stand,
The bridge constructed by his hand."
Saying so he disappeared,
The ocean that Prince Raghav seared.
Nala filled his task with love,
Blessed by all the gods above.
Ten leagues wide and hundred long,
That causeway was immense and strong.
From start to end it took six days,
And all the siddhas sang their praise.
With rocks and trees they built the bridge,
Like a massive, floating ridge.
Happily the banars leapt
As they across the causeway swept.
Some did swim and some did fly,
Among them their morale was high.
Soon they reached the island shore,
And set up camp to strength restore.
Secretly the gods did bless,
Affection did they all profess,
That Ram would rule eternally,
To rule the earth and rule the sea.

23

The omens of the land foretold
A battle lurked, both rash and bold.
The quaking earth and dusty storm,
Did of danger them inform.
Blood did shower from the sky,
And birds and beasts did moan and cry.

Without delay they stood to fight,
Those banars of impressive might.

24

The banars stood in their formation,
Each awaiting at their station.
Drums and gongs from Lanka rolled,
The coming of a war it told.
And all the banars gave a roar,
They who reached the northern shore.
Then sighing, Ram to Lakshman spoke
The feelings that in him awoke:
"Magnificent, this citadel,
Where groves and birds and cuckoos dwell,
Whose palaces do touch the sky,
As if within the clouds they fly."
The troops were marshalled to the fore,
As if they knocked at Lanka's door.
Shuka was by them set free
And quickly to his king did flee.
With fettered wings and mangled flesh,
The banars did of him enmesh:
"There is no way to mediate
With banar men that brachiate
They threw a bridge across the sea,
Traversing here in search of thee.
Bhalukas do clog the earth,
Tall in height and wide in girth.
Now decide how you will act;
Sally forth or now retract."
But Ravan, proud of empty might
Resolved that he would Raghav fight.
Believing none could challenge him,
Even less he thought of them.

25

Ravan then dispatched two spies,
Of the foe they would apprise.
In the form of banars went,
Those spies that Ravan there had sent.
But Bibhishan saw their disguise,
And thought to apprehend them wise.
They sought protection at the feet
Of Ram, of whom they did entreat.
And Ram did let them freely see
The army in entirety,
Then set them free to meet their king
And news of Raghav's prowess bring.
To Ravan they gave full report,
And of Ram's courage, gave support.
They said that they could not defeat
Raghav, nor could they compete.
Maithili they should return,
But Ravan did their counsel spurn.

26

Sāraṇa described the host
Of banars, as each one did boast
That Lanka, by him would be laid
To waste; this boast each one had made.
They gnashed their teeth and lashed their tails,
Foamed and growled and issued wails.
Infinite their forces stood,
The onslaught could not be withstood.
Sugriva, Nila, Angada,
Nala, Rambha, Kumuda,
Kanda and Samrocana,
Sharabha and Krathana—
These warriors did stand to fight,
Each resplendent in his might.

Huge of stance and firm of gaze,
These banars in their strength did blaze.

27

"The Lord of Bhalukas is there,
With ebony and sable hair.
Large as mountains, they can toss
A boulder like a piece of dross.
A league in width and height is he,
Sannādana, of bravery.
Indra could not him defeat,
Such the prowess of his feat.
With coiled tails and thunderous roars,
These banars have obscured our shores.
Of copper, black, and honey hue,
These banars one cannot subdue.
Agile, virile, strong and brave,
These banars pose a danger grave."

28

Now Shuka did resume discourse
About this endless banar force:
"Born of gods, the banars change
Their form, and freely thus do range.
Immortal wine some have obtained,
And now you are by them detained.
Hanuman to us returned,
The one who had our city burned.
And that man of bluish skin,
Where lotus eyes do dwell within,
Versed in scripture, firm in vows,
He who now your death avows,
Has sallied forth to fight with thee,
For his consort, Maithili.
And on his right with hue of gold,
Is Lakshman, ever brave and bold.

Devoted to his brother's good,
His loyalty is understood.
And on his left is Bibhishan,
Who with the banars marches on.
Raghunanda thus installs
Him as king when Lanka falls.
Sugriva wears the golden chain
Where Lakshmi and good fortune reign.
Countless banars gather here
And each is brave, bereft of fear.
Prepare thyself to wage a war,
For Raghav has a vengeance swore."

29

As volcanoes do erupt,
So Ravan's ire became abrupt.
Unpleasant news they dared to bring
Unto a vain and selfish king.
Because of service rendered past,
They were spared their lives at last.
Ravan called for better spies,
And sent them to Sri Ram apprise.
But they were apprehended there,
Bibhishan could see their snare.
Raghav let the spies go free,
And they returned most hastily.

30

Shardula to him reported,
How these banars with him sported.
Beaten, bitten, kicked and punched,
He was by those banars crunched.
Ram released and set him free,
So he returned there shamefully.
Either Sita they return,
Or sally forth for battle yearn.

But Ravan did refuse to yield;
He preferred his mace to wield.

31

Intent to gain the upper hand,
Ravan acted as he planned.
By his nature he was cruel
And sought to trick Prince Raghav's jewel.
By the power of illusion,
Suffering from his delusion,
Craftsmen did he so instruct,
The head of Raghav to construct.
Bow and arrows should he bring
Resembling those of Sita's king.
Janaki, by him deceived,
The death of Ram she had believed.
To Ashoka grove he went,
His thoughts on Janaki intent.
Beneath the tree, upon the ground,
Vaidehi was by Ravan found.
And with his wily pantomime,
The death of Ram did Ravan chime:
"Oh lady of the slender waist,
Thou who art forever chaste,
I bring you news you long to hear,
That your lord has now come near.
With his banar host he camped,
Upon our shores they wailed and stamped.
My titans issued forth at night,
And valiantly that host did smite.
Prahasta did remove the head
Of Ram and now your lord is dead.
Sugriva's neck by him was snapped,
All of them by us were trapped.
Hanuman was also slain,
Their battle was completely vain.

Everywhere they ran to hide,
Those banars ran on every side.
Bibhishan we did arrest,
And Lakshman fled with all the rest.
Defenseless, thou did wait in vain,
Now next to me you have to reign."
He called his servant there to bring
The severed head of Sita's king.
He threw the head at Sita's feet,
Misguiding her with cruel deceit.
He raised the bow aloft and cried,
That now she would with him abide.

32

Like an osprey Sita wailed,
When she saw the head unveiled:
"Now Kaikeyi is content
Since Raghav's life has now been spent."
She trembled and fell to the earth,
She of an auspicious birth.
When her senses were regained,
Her lamentations thereby rained:
"What misery does overwhelm
This creature like a broken helm.
The greatest misery in life
Is when the lord precedes his wife
In death, and she is left alone,
Left to cry a silent moan.
How could you precede me there?
To leave me thus, you should not dare.
Why do you refuse me here,
Oh Prince Raghav, mine so dear?
Oh cruel Ranger of the Night,
Now my life do also smite,
To reunite my lord in death,
I forsake my vital breath."

Then a demon told the king
That Prahasta news did bring.
Urgently the titans left
As Vaidehi grieved and wept.
And when he left it disappeared,
The head of Ram that she had feared.
Then Ravan's forces did he call;
Prepared for war, they would not stall.

33

One female titan there consoled
Vaidehi, who in grief had rolled.
Ravan used deceitful means,
Illusion wrapped his evil skeins.
Ram and Lakshman were alive,
And at the shore they did arrive.
Soon the war with them would start,
Vaidehi should be strong of heart.
Reunited she would be,
Raghav with sweet Maithili.

34

Sarama addressed that queen,
A pearl among all jewels unseen,
And offered to a message send
To Sri Ram, upon the wind.
But Maithili did ask of her
The plans of Ravan to secure,
And let her know how he would act,
And so they made a secret pact.
On that monarch did she spy,
And back to Sita did she fly.
The mother of that titan king,
Said that he should Sita bring
With honor to the Best of Men,
This battle they could never win.

But Ravan would not let her go,
Thus the seed of death did sow.
As she spoke the banars cheered,
The titans heard what they had feared.

35

Malyavan, the king's grandsire,
Listened to the banar's ire.
For Ravan's benefit he spoke,
But contempt it did provoke.
He counseled him to send her back,
And thus avoid a vain attack.
All the omens did portend
Annihilation at their end.
Yama did the king deceive,
For Janaki he would not leave.

36

Ravan closed his ears and eyes
To counsel given by the wise,
Finding no significance
To Raghav's feat but only chance.
So he did his fort defend
With soldiers placed at every end.

37

Ram with his advisors met,
Their plan of action then was set.
Their spies returned from Lanka where
Their course of action could compare.
Ram reserved the right to slay
Ravan in this awesome fray.
So they proceeded to their post,
That vast array of banar host.

38

Raghav, Lakshman, Bibhishan,
Sugriva, also Hanuman,
Did Suvela Mount ascend
Surveying Lanka to its end.
The sun descended in the west,
And there the heroes stayed to rest.

39

With the freshness of the day,
In readiness they did array.
The beauty of the fort was seen,
By the rays the sun did preen.
Set atop a mountain crest,
The city was in glory dressed.
The banars stamped and raised a dust,
They were brave and quite robust.

40

From Mount Suvela they could see
Ravan on his balcony.
Like a cloud of reddened hue,
Ravan made the earth askew.
As Sugriva did perceive,
The rage within did surge and heave.
And with a bound to there he flew,
And face to face did him pursue.
Fiercely the two did struggle,
Beating each with fisted cudgel.
Smeared with blood, each one did fight,
Ferociously they used their might.
Ravan wearied in the fray,
Sugriva did that titan stay.
He bounded high into the air,
And landed with Prince Raghav there,

Increasing Raghav's pure delight,
Because he did with Ravan fight.

41

Raghav gently chided him
For the rash display of vim.
But when Sugriva saw that creature
He reacted by his nature.
Winds of Time upon them swept
And evil omens near them crept,
Foreboding many soon would die,
Their bodies on the earth to lie.
They advanced to Lanka's gate,
And cautiously they did there wait.
Each one took up his position
Stationed at his own division.
Banars waited in their ranks,
They gnashed their teeth and lashed their flanks.
Lanka did they all surround,
With bhalukas upon the ground.
And when the demons saw their foe,
Terror filled their minds with woe.
Raghav called to Bāli's son
To enter Lanka, fearing none,
And his message to deliver
That he is the earth's lawgiver.
Angada leapt in the air
And landed next to Ravan there.
Like a torch within the dark
Angada did anger spark:
"The son of Bāli, I am known,
My valor shall to you be shown.
A messenger I come to thee
From Ram, who holds thy destiny:
'Come fight with me, thou wretched scourge,
Soon the life of thee I'll purge.

Bibhishan will next be king,
When you to death I quickly bring.
Cast thyself upon my feet,
And mercy from me do entreat.
Return my consort graciously,
Or fight with me capriciously'."
Like a maddened dog that barks,
Inflamed by Angada's remarks,
Ravan uttered with his breath
To seize him and put him to death,
But Angada three titans held
And with a bound he quickly felled
Those demons, setting them to nought,
And then the palace top he sought.
By the power of his bound,
The palace crumbled to the ground.
And like an eagle in the air
He flew to meet Prince Raghav there.
The banar host did cheer with pride,
The demons were afraid inside,
And both the sides advanced to fight,
Summoning their fierce might.

42

Lanka was by them besieged,
By banars who with Ram were lieged.
The walls were battered with the trees
And rocks the banars threw with ease.
The arches, ramparts, walls, and moat,
The banars with their fists had smote
And scaled the walls, did demons toss
Into the moat, like floating dross.
"Victory to Ram" they cried,
As they did in battle ride.
Every gate by them was blocked,
Every exit they had locked.

But from within the fortress wall,
Ravan did a sortie call,
And drums and trumpets from there blared,
As Ravan, bright with anger, glared.
Everywhere did soldiers roar,
And bodies lay like sandy shore.
The titans fought with hook and spear,
And with harpoon, their foes did sear.
Ferociously each one did fight,
Intent upon each one to smite.

43

The chariots rolled on the field,
And darts and arrows did they wield,
And elephants crushed underneath
The banars like a morbid wreath.
From their corpses blood did flow,
And their hair, like grass, did grow.
Their chariots by fists were shattered,
And the drivers' blood had splattered.
Maces riven in the chest
Bade their foes with death to wrest.
And arrows pierced banar flesh,
As they with trees and rocks did thresh.
Heads were severed by the wheels
Of chariots like mortal seals.
Eyes were scratched and heads were crushed
As each upon the other rushed.
A fearful carnage there ensued,
Where headless trunks on earth were skewed.
Night befell that awful field,
Where death his rod did freely wield.

44

Even though the night did fall,
The fighting 'twixt them did not pall.

The night did all their faces mask,
So each his race did have to ask.
The smell of blood did drive them mad
To eat the flesh of those they had,
And they were favored in the night,
Those demons did enhance their might.
The banars with their teeth and claws,
Gouged their eyes, their chests, and jaws.
Blood did flow in rushing rivers,
As the arrows left their quivers.
Gongs and drums and conches blew,
And chariots did rattle through.
The shafts of Ram illumed the night,
The field of battle was their light.
Like moths that rush into a flame,
The demons did pursue the same.
Angada of awesome might
Gave Indrajit a savage fight
Who resorted to black art,
Invisible, he did depart.
Angada by all was hailed,
For over him he had prevailed.
Indrajit did boil within,
And took revenge on those two men.
Invisible within the sky,
His arrows on those two did fly,
And Ram and Lakshman did he wrap
With serpents from his evil trap.

45

The banars leapt into the air
To try to find the demon there,
But he did lacerate them all
With shafts that from his bow did fall.
His wrath was lashed upon the prince,
And broke the bow of Raghav hence.

Every inch of flesh did wrap
With darts and arrows from his trap.
And Lakshman, too, received the same;
Both were senseless and were lame.

46

They on a bed of arrows lay,
Bathed in blood, their breath did stay.
The banars greatly did lament
The fateful turn of this event.
Indrajit announced his feat,
That he the Raghus did defeat.
And all the titans cheered and hailed
That demon who black arts had veiled.
Then ruthlessly he pierced his foe,
And all their ranks were filled with woe.
Hidden in the cloak of night,
That demon did perversely fight
And laughed aloud amidst the cloud,
He who was by nature proud.
Stationed at the demon's head,
Indrajit said 'Ram is dead.'
As the fog rolls on the lake,
Sugriva did in terror shake,
But Bibhishan retained the force,
That fate had not yet run its course.
Bibhishan erased his fears,
And Sugriva's bitter tears,
And told him with resolve to face
The bane of Ramachandra's race.
Indrajit informed his sire,
The Raghus did at last expire.

47

With a cruel and mean delight,
That Ranger of the Bitter Night,

Forced Vaidehi to the field
To see her lord to death did yield.
There did Ram and Lakshman lay,
Vanquished in this bitter fray.
Ravan to Vaidehi said,
Her lord and master now was dead.

48

When Sita saw their life did part,
The dam of grief broke in her heart,
And she bewailed her bitter fate,
That such an end did her await.
Her body bore auspicious signs,
Nowhere had she widow lines,
And she remembered Raghav's mother,
Lost to grief and one another.
But Trijata told her there
That she should not her soul despair.
The faces of the heroes glow,
Life within them did it show,
And all the troops did still array,
Panic did not them belay.
She told Vaidehi to be strong,
The struggle still was on and long.

49

Ram did from his swoon awake,
But Lakshman's visage made him quake.
Bitter grief did rack his soul,
And Lakshman's virtues did extol.
A wife one always can replace,
But one cannot a brother trace.
What is kingdom or his wife,
Without Lakshman, what is life?
He told Sugriva to retreat,
He was happy with his feat.

And all the banars with him cried
To see Prince Lakshman at his side.

50

Like rats upon a sinking ship,
The banars did retreat and skip,
When a titan did approach,
Whom they thought a fight did broach.
But it was only Bibhishan
From whom they did retreat and run.
Jamwant rallied each one back
For Bibhishan did not attack.
Bibhishan with grief perceived
Those heroes whom the arrows weaved.
With his hands he washed their eyes,
Lamenting both in their demise.
They on whom he did depend,
Now no longer could defend.
And Ravan did attain his end,
By vanquishing his human friend.
Sugriva told them all to heed,
That Ram and Lakshman would succeed.
A fierce wind around them blew,
And trees and rocks together flew.
Garuda did to them appear,
And all the serpents fled in fear.
Garuda did their bodies stroke,
And from the swoon they both awoke.
Their wounds did heal upon his touch,
For he so loved them overmuch.
All their strength did then return,
The vigor in their veins did burn.
Lovingly he Ram embraced,
Selflessly his love effaced.
Raghav asked his unknown friend,
Why he did so serve his end?

As on the wind, a feather flies,
So his breath with Ram now lies.
The mystery would be revealed,
When Ram succeeds on battlefield.
He vanished with the speed of thought,
And all the banars there were fraught
With glee as they did leap and roar,
Ready to wage war some more.

51

Like the toll of death that wails,
Ravan heard the fierce hails,
Full of revelry and cheer,
For Ram and Lakshman did appear.
Ravan did uneasy grow,
When he heard them make a row
And sent his troops to ascertain
From where they did this vigor gain.
They informed their titan king
That to life they both did spring.
Full of vigor, they did flow
Freed from venom and its throe.
With trepidation, Ravan sent
Dhumraksha with evil bent.
With his army he went out
But evil omens gave him doubt.
Vultures landed on his car,
And raining blood his face did mar.
Headless trunks before him fell,
And hopeless cries arose from hell.

52

The titans entered in the fray
And countless banars they did stay
With spears and maces, shafts, and ax;
The banars did in wrath soon wax.

And with their trees, their teeth and nail,
Many titans they did flail.
Though pierced with those shafts and spear,
The banars fought them, lacking fear.
They tore their flesh with teeth and nail,
And crushed them as the demons wail.
Elephants and horses died
In heaps like mountains on their side.
They pulled their hair and scratched their eyes
And crushed them in between their thighs.
The banars did the titans rout,
Dhumraksha then gave a shout.
A fierce carnage did ensue,
When Dhumraksha did them pursue.
Their chests and entrails by him slashed,
Hanuman in anger flashed.
He crushed his car and killed his steed,
And leapt on him with agile speed.
With a mountain peak he raised,
Dhumraksha to earth was razed.
Then all the titans quickly fled;
Dhumraksha they saw was dead.

53

Ravan did in fury hiss,
When his plan had gone amiss.
Vajradamshtra next he sent
To slay Sri Ram he was intent.
With his army he filed out,
But evil portents were about.
A fiery vomit jackals cast,
As those titans fought their last
Battle with the banar host,
As on their lips success they'd boast.
A savage fight therein ensued
And headless trunks the field pursued.

Hand-to-hand they each did fight,
Each the other tried to smite.
Angada and Hanuman
Sent the titans on the run.

54

Vajradamshtra rose in fury
As the titans 'round did scurry.
Vultures, crows, and jackals ate
The flesh of those succumbed to fate.
Headless trunks ran through the field,
And terror to them all did yield.
The demon's eyes were red with wrath
Who made the field a bloody bath.
The demon fought with Bāli's son
And fiery tongues on him were spun,
Then Angada did hurl a tree—
The demon broke it easily.
Angada his car did smash,
Then hand-to-hand the two did clash.
With mace and fist the two did fight,
Like the darkness and the light.
Besmeared with blood and gaping wound,
To their knees they both had swooned.
But Angada leapt in a flash
And with his sword his head did slash.
Cleft in two, the titan fell,
And all the demons fled pell-mell.
Honored by the banar host,
Of this feat they all did boast.

55

Akampan next he did deploy
To the banar host destroy.
His division followed course,
Intent to slay the banar force.

He rattled forth like rolling thunder,
As he cleft them all asunder,
Evil omens crossed his way,
But he would not from duty sway.
From their cruel and savage fight,
The dust arose like sable night.
And none could see his friend or foes,
And blindly gave each other blows.
Banars fought among their kind,
And titans with their own entwined.
The dust did settle into mud
Drenched with all the gore and blood.
Viciously they each did fight,
The banar men displayed their might.
The titan army they did rout,
Triumphantly they all did shout.

56

Akampan this could not abide,
And to the foray did he ride.
With his shafts he smote the foe,
Spears and darts and ax did throw.
Through the field he drove his car,
And all the banars he did mar.
Then Hanuman did go to where
Those banars filled with grave despair.
Myriads of shafts did fall
On Hanuman, as he stood tall.
He laughed aloud and blazed with ire,
Resplendent like a smokeless fire.
He spun a rock upon his hand,
But before that rock could land,
Akampan soon dissolved it there,
As his shafts flew through the air.
Then a tree he whirled around
Demolishing all that he found.

Akampan pierced all his flesh,
And Hanuman he did enmesh.
But with a bound he struck his head,
Akampan then at last was dead.
The titans fled in each direction,
Lanka offered them protection.
Hanuman with praise was laid,
By the leaders and brigade.
The devas did extol his name,
The Son of Wind accrued great fame.

57

Next, Prahasta did emerge,
As if he could the banars purge.
With great pomp he left the gate,
But jackals did that one await.
Evil omens did portend
A swiftness to Prahasta's end.
His horses stumbled on the land,
And reins fell from his driver's hand.
The banars did prepare to fight
Those titans of tremendous might.

58

Prahasta like a fury came,
And many banars did he maim.
The gates of death he then did flood,
With the rivers of their blood.
But Nila could not tolerate
The carnage he did mediate.
Advancing like a great typhoon,
Nila did that titan prune.
He pierced Nila with his dart,
But Nila bore it, firm of heart.
With a tree he killed his horse,
His car, and driver, with great force.

They faced each other on the ground,
Both whose prowess was renowned.
Prahasta struck the banar's head,
But Nila crushed the demon dead.
Blood gushed forth like many fountains
Down the sides of terraced mountains.
Then to Lanka they had fled
Terrorized to see him dead.
Felicitations were received
By Nila for the deed achieved.

59

Ravan did himself decide,
That he would to battle ride.
Surrounded by his valiant men,
Confident that he would win.
Majestic in his slow approach,
Brilliant like a diamond broach,
Ravan did great awe inspire,
He who supplicated fire.
As soon as Ravan entered there,
Sugriva bounded in the air,
And with a mountain peak aside,
He threw it at that monarch's pride.
Ravan swiftly shattered that
And with a missile loosed it at
Sugriva with a deadly aim,
And Ravan did that banar maim.
All the titans cheered with pride,
The banar host did they deride.
The generals rushed to his aid,
But Ravan all their efforts stayed,
And rained upon that vast array
Of banars, shafts that never stray.
To Ram the banars quickly fled,
Ravan's anger did they dread.

But Lakshman did beseech his friend
To let him bring that demon's end.
Then Hanuman beheld that king,
Whose shafts the noose of death did bring.
Hanuman did threaten him,
That his death did wait with them.
The mighty blows their fist did cleave,
Beneath the weight, each one did heave.
Ravan did that banar strike,
And he reeled beneath his might.
Ravan turned his car around
On Nila, did his weapons bound.
Rocks and trees that banar threw,
But Ravan did them quickly hew.
He broke the trees within his hand,
Sifting them like blocks of sand.
Many shafts he then did shower
On that general of power.
Nila quickly changed his form,
Like a mouse he did transform.
On his standard did he leap,
Then to his banner did he peep.
Then he jumped onto his bow,
There his suppleness did show.
He leapt about and gave a shout,
And Ravan was confused throughout.
On his diadem he tarried,
King of Titans, Nila, carried.
They began to cheer and laugh
To see him dancing on his staff.
Infuriated, Ravan drew
The shaft of fire to him pursue.
The shaft did pierce Nila's chest,
And his senses did arrest.
But Nila born of hallowed fire,
Was protected by his sire.

Then Lakshman did approach that king
Who was prone to quarreling,
To enter in the fray with men,
He should taste their wrath therein.
Their arrows on each other rained,
But none's advantage could be gained.
Then with a shaft from Brahma's hand,
On Lakshman did that arrow land.
But Lakshman had regained his sense,
And Ravan's bow did he dispense.
Then Lakshman now harassed his foe,
With shafts that did some havoc sow.
Battered and besmeared with blood,
The wrath of Ravan's dam did flood.
A spear from Brahma he received
There on Lakshman it had cleaved,
And senseless on the ground did swoon,
Vanquished by the Grandsire's boon.
Ravan had perversely seized
Lakshman, as he senseless wheezed.
But he could not that Raghu budge,
He could not his body nudge.
The essence of the Lord was he,
Bound to Ram eternally.
Then Hanuman leapt to his aid,
And smote him with the fist he made,
And Ravan reeled beneath that blow,
Delivered by his mortal foe.
Then Lakshman had that banar raised
By his lightness, was amazed,
For his love did lightly carry
He on whom the earth did tarry.
Spears returned to Ravan's hold
And once again he grew too bold.
Lakshman from that blow recovered,
His true nature was discovered.

Swiftly through the field did stride
That banar whom Sri Ram did ride.
Ram did call that demon king
To stay, his death to him would bring.
At Hanuman his shafts did fly,
The rage within did grow and cry.
Ram then with an arrow crushed
His chariot, as Ravan rushed.
Then with a dart he struck his chest,
And Ravan was by it distressed.
And with a shaft he broke his crown,
As Ravan did in anger frown.
Raghunanda gave reprieve,
That Ravan should for Lanka leave.
Humbled and deprived of pride,
Ravan did to Lanka ride.
All the devas did rejoice,
Hailing Raghav in one voice.

60

Ravan's wrath was quite provoked,
As his hate for Ram he stoked.
Humbled by Prince Raghav's strength,
He would go to any length
To vanquish him and take his life,
And make Vaidehi be his wife.
The King of Titans called a meeting,
Scheming of Sri Ram defeating.
Kumbhakarn did lie asleep,
But for his prowess they did weep.
Kumbhakarn they would awake,
For Ravan's life was now at stake.
With food and garlands, sandalpaste,
Titans scurried with all haste
To waken that gigantic one
Who slumbered while deceit was spun.

Upon the ground that giant lay,
In his cave for months to stay,
His mouth agape like doors of hell,
And he of blood and filth did smell.
The tunnels of his nostrils heaved
As that monster deeply breathed,
And pressed them back against the wall
They who were as mountains tall.
Gold and jewels adorned the floor,
As the thunder, did he snore.
They did flesh before him pile,
And canisters of blood and bile
To stave his hunger when he woke,
So as not to ire provoke.
They rubbed his skin with scented paste,
And sang his praises in their haste.
They blew their horns and beat his chest;
To rouse him they did try their best,
But he from sleep could not awake,
Even though they did him shake.
Elephants and camels trod
Upon him, like an earthen clod.
They roared and shouted at his head,
But he remained as one who's dead.
Then those titans were inflamed,
And Kumbhakarn they even maimed.
They pulled his hair and bit his ears,
Stabbed him with their sharpened spears,
Ten thousand demons trampled hard,
Then suddenly he felt this shard.
He yawned and as his mouth did gape,
The gates of hell within took shape.
They motioned to the food they kept
To feed him after he had slept.
Ravenous, he was complete
As soon as he did eat the meat.

He drank the blood and ate the fat,
And there among them he had sat.
Kumbhakarn inquired of them,
Why they did so waken him.
The counsellors to him replied,
That Ravan did from battle ride.
Raghav had defeated them,
They were sent to waken him.
They brought him endless crates of wine
To drink, and flesh on which to dine.
To Ravan's palace did he go,
The foes of him to overthrow.
From the field the banars saw
That giant, who filled all with awe.
In their terror they did flee
In all directions hastily.

61

Astonished at his mammoth size,
Raghav asked in great surprise,
Who could this apparition be,
Whose sight caused all his troops to flee?
Bibhishan did answer him,
With words where truth and honor brim:
"Kumbhakarn, my father's son,
Is he from whom our troops do run.
He is his own authority,
From that springs his pugnacity.
The gods could not that one defeat,
So they the Grandsire did entreat.
As soon as Kumbhakarn was born,
The beings from the earth were torn,
There he soon devoured their flesh,
And their bones by him did mesh.
He struck Devendra in a fight,
And vanquished him with simple might.

To Brahmadeva they did flee,
To save them from calamity.
And Brahmadeva in his turn,
Kumbhakarn he did so spurn,
And sleep lay on him as one dead,
This curse he laid upon his head.
At once he fell into a swoon,
But Ravan did request a boon
That Brahma should decide a time
When Kumbhakarn from sleep could climb.
So every six months does he wake,
For just one day his thirst can slake
And ravish through the earthly floor,
To search for flesh and eat some more.
Now that giant is awake,
In fear of you, the demons quake.
Our troops should now together hold,
And face the foe together, bold."
The ranks were rallied and began
To seize the fort as they did plan.

62

Kumbhakarn approached that king
To ascertain why he did bring
That colossus to his throne,
He wanted him to make it known.
Ravan said his adversary
Vanquished them, and they were wary.
He remained their only hope,
To fight with Ram they could not cope.
Kumbhakarn, without delay,
Said he would Prince Raghav slay.

63

Kumbhakarn did know the source
Of why events did take this course.

When one does act without a pause,
And does not reason for the cause,
In jeopardy he'll find his way,
And by the tides of fate will sway.
Every season has its turn,
One does not the other spurn.
Acting out of consequence,
Leaves one prey to circumstance.
Without discernment of the cause,
The fruits will snare you in their claws.
Disregarding sound advice
Can leave one in the grips of vice.
A selfish king can only rule
By the acts both mean and cruel.
Now the tides did turn again
And Ravan was the prey of men.
Ravan did not want to hear
The words from those who held him dear.
Angrily his wrath ignited
As his gaze on him alighted.
Ravan did not want to know
He had to reap what he did sow.
Within the present circumstance,
What should be their martial stance,
Is why that monarch called him there,
To save him from his grave despair.
Regardless of his impudence,
How to stop this turbulence?
So Kumbhakarn affirmed the fact,
War is what he would transact.
And lay to waste that banar host,
So he did to Ravan boast.

64

Mahodara said to him,
Kumbhakarn, the best of them,

That Ram he could not face alone,
His power still remained unknown.
Impetuously did he speak,
Doing so his death would seek.
Together they should face the foe,
And deal to him a deathly blow.
Or they could spin a cruel deceit
To bring Vaidehi to their feet,
Convincing her that Ram was dead,
Her fears and sorrows by them fed.

65

Kumbhakarn dispelled his speech
Convinced his arms could overreach
And slay Prince Raghav in the field
By the force his arms could wield.
Ravan honored him, his brother,
And they did embrace each other.
Kumbhakarn prepared to fight
And evil portents came to light.
Disregarding every sign,
The army marched with him in line.
And when the banars saw him come,
Their terror made their senses numb.
Kumbhakarn did sneer and laugh,
As he wrote his epitaph.

66

Over Lanka's wall he leapt,
And with a furor he had swept
Bhalukas and banars there
To the realm of Yama's snare.
The banars in their fear did flee,
Some did jump into the sea.
Some did fly to seek protection,
Others ran in each direction.

Angada did try his best
To rally all the forces lest
They be known in infamy,
For cowardice, this infantry.
But Kumbhakarn did lay them waste,
They ran from him in fear and haste.

67

With Angada's courageous word
They faced the titan undeterred.
But Kumbhakarn did wield his mace
And many did that one displace,
As thirty at a time he crushed
And ate, as he in battle rushed.
Hanuman stood in the air,
Raining rocks into his hair,
But Kumbhakarn was unperturbed,
The onslaught had not him disturbed.
His body streamed with blood and fat,
From the banar flesh he spat.
Hanuman did strike his chest
And Kumbhakarn did he arrest.
Then that colossus threw his spear,
As all the banars fled in fear,
And Hanuman received that blow,
As blood from out his mouth did flow.
Banars clung unto their foe,
But he did not so feel their blow.
He crushed them as they fell around,
Then all the banars did surround
That titan like a tower high,
And thousands on him then did fly.
He crushed and ate that banar rank,
His mouth agape, of death it stank,
And from his ears and nose they ran,
As entrails on his ears did fan.

Angada did try to halt
Kumbhakarn's depraved assault,
And with a blow he smote his chest
And for a moment did arrest
That monster, who then struck his foe,
And senselessly fell from that blow.
Then Kumbhakarn beheld the King
Of Banars, as he then did spring
And fiercely did battle wage
Igniting both their ire and rage.
A spear of lightning in his hand,
The titan meant for it to land
On Sugriva's broadened chest,
But Hanuman did it arrest,
And broke that spear across his knee,
As if it were a brittle tree.
Then Kumbhakarn became incensed,
And with a mountain peak dispensed
A blow upon Sugriva, hence
He fell to earth, bereft of sense.
He seized Sugriva and returned
To Lanka, when that banar turned
And tore his thighs and nose and ear,
And with a bound, to Ram was near.
Kumbhakarn, by now enraged,
A vicious war upon them waged.
Driven by his lust for meat
All beside him did he eat
Trying to appease his hunger,
Friend or foe succumbed to danger.
Maddened by the smell of blood,
The dam of hunger did him flood.
Lakshman did ascend the fight
And sallied forth with all his might.
Kumbhakarn was gratified
By the strength he verified,

But the shafts did that one swallow
By his girth, like one who's hollow.
Disregarding Lakshman's arm,
Which failed to cause him any harm,
To Sri Ram he rushed to fight,
Intent he could Prince Raghav smite.
Ram did now infuriate
With the shafts he did create,
That demon who now dropped his weapons,
As Lord Yama's shadow beckons.
Foe or friend he did not know,
And killed them with his crushing blow.
Banars by the thousands flung
Themselves at him, and to him clung.
Kumbhakarn did vomit blood,
The rains of which the field did flood.
Raghav's shafts on him did quench,
From their blows he did not flinch.
Kumbhakarn had raised his mace,
But Ram a deadly shaft did place
And loosed it at that demon's limb,
The titan's arm was lost by him.
He screamed and through the worlds it fell,
That echo from the depths of hell.
Then Sri Ram the other severed,
Yet the titan still endeavored,
Trying to attack the prince,
He who was deprived of sense.
With two shafts he cut his feet,
But Kumbhakarn would not retreat.
He rushed on Ram with mouth agape;
With arrows, Ram his mouth did tape.
Senseless he sat on the ground,
Unable to emit a sound.
A brilliant missile filled the sky
With searing light as it did fly.

And all the heavens filled with light,
As it did that demon smite.
His head was severed from his trunk,
His body in the sea was sunk.
His head fell on the city's wall,
He who once had stood so tall.
Then the heavens did rejoice,
Lauding Ram in single voice.
Lanka was succumbed to grief,
None from fear could find relief.

68

The news of Kumbhakarn's own death
Now left Ravan out of breath.
He who was his life's support,
Raghav did to death deport.
Useless had his life become
When his brother did succumb.

69

The sons of Ravan did propose
To enter combat with his foes.
Skilled in magic, they could fly,
On their boons they did rely.
Never had they known defeat,
The gods could not with them compete.
Brothers of the titan king
Sallied forth, their death to bring.
Every weapon, every steed,
Was provided for their need.
Adorned with golden armor, they
Were resplendent like the day.
Mighty chariots they rode,
Prompted by Lord Yama's goad.
Resolved to conquer or to die,
Their shouts of joy shook the sky.

The titan army charged the field,
And every weapon did they wield.
The banar host replied in kind
With trees and boulders they could find.
The banars and the titans fought,
The death of each the other sought.
They roared like lions in the field,
Resolved to fight, they would not yield.
Mountains of their corpses grew,
Friend or foe they both did hew.
Severed limbs became their rod,
As underfoot they entrails trod.
They swung the corpses like the trees,
To smite their foes with agile ease.
The banars did the titans rout,
But soon events did turn about.
Narantaka did draw his spear,
Whose brilliance did the banars sear.
Like a conflagration he
Consumed their forces easily.
His stroke was like a lightning bolt,
None of them could stand the jolt.
Soon they ran in each direction,
Failing to find some protection.
King Sugriva saw this fight
And sent Angada there to smite
That warrior, most speedily,
For him it would come easily.
Without a weapon he approached
Narantaka and him reproached.
Narantaka did thrust his spear
At Angada, who had no fear,
And it was shattered on his chest,
As if he did with toys jest.
Angada struck down his steed,
But that titan did not heed,

And struck that banar on his crown
Senseless, he was smitten down.
But Angada regained his sense,
And with a blow did he dispense
That titan to the realm of death,
Deprived of glory and of breath.
The devas did acclaim the name
Of Angada, increasing fame.

70

Trishirā and Devantaka,
Together fought Prince Angada,
And Mahodara also fought,
The death of Bāli's son they sought.
Yet Angada remained unmoved;
His tremendous strength it proved.
The elephant he soon did kill,
Testifying of his skill,
And pulling out that mammoth tusk
He fought with them in manner brusque.
Hanuman and Nila rushed
To help Angada's foes be crushed.
Many were the trees they threw,
But their shafts cut them in two.
Devantaka with mace in hand,
Raised his arms, a blow to land,
But Hanuman that fight did win,
And crushed his skull, his eyes, and chin.
Many were the shafts he showered
As Trishirā overpowered
Nila, with his uncle's aid,
Mahodara led the raid.
But Nila did regain his sense,
And Mahodara did dispense,
By crushing him beneath a rock,
The blow of which caused earth a shock.

Trishirā was inflamed with rage,
On Hanuman his ire did wage.
Like a meteor it flew
The spear Trishirā on him threw.
But Hanuman did break that spear
And all the banar host did cheer.
Then with his sword he stabbed his breast,
He who was the banar's best.
But Hanuman did slap him down
And seized the titan by his crown,
And with a single stroke he cut
His three heads, like a coconut.
The titans' ire did foam and steam,
Their fiery wrath caused blood to stream.
Matta and Rishabha fought,
And finally Rishabha brought
The brother of the king to death,
Depriving him of his life-breath.

71

Upon his car that titan came,
Who throughout had gathered fame
For skill and prowess, chastity,
Endowed with great sagacity.
Skillful in the art of war,
Celestial weapons with him bore,
Procured through Bramadeva's favor,
Wisdom and respect did savor.
Armor was invincible,
His brilliance, indivisible.
The gods could not defeat this one,
He had all the battles won.
Atikaya was his name,
And all the worlds did him acclaim.
That titan did the banars rout,
They could not withstand his clout.

He challenged Ram to come and fight,
Lesser men had little might.
But Lakshman did address that foe,
And bravely stood with shaft and bow.
The titan told him to be gone,
A child he would not light upon.
Lakshman stood his ground the same,
Defiantly called out his name.
A fierce struggle did ensue
As they tried to each subdue.
Equal in their might, they fought,
Though each the other's death had sought.
Both were wounded, both were strong,
The battle lasted very long.
The heavens glowed with brilliant light,
From the missiles in the fight.
Celestial weapons, mantra-born,
By the other's shaft was shorn.
But Atikaya was protected
From the shafts the prince trajected.
What he wore could not be torn,
It was from the Grandsire born.
Lakshman loosed Lord Brahma's dart,
The heavens in surprise did start.
It severed Atikaya's head,
Which fell unto its earthly bed.
The titans were distraught with fear,
Dropping every shaft and spear.
The devas did the feat applaud,
And hymns of praise on him did laud.

72

His sons and brothers now were dead,
But Ravan could not look ahead.
Beset by anguish and by grief,
Ravan there found no relief.

The gates and ramparts fortified,
Ravan did reflect inside.

73

Indrajit resolved to fight
The banars and the Raghus smite.
The titan army sought to win,
Armed with sword and javelin.
Indrajit invoked the fire,
And their destruction did conspire.
His offerings the fire consumed,
Victory it did presume.
The Brahma weapon he invoked,
A smokeless flame it had evoked.
Indrajit did disappear;
Invisible, he courted fear.
In the sky he stood unseen
And loosed his arrows very keen.
The banar force he did assault,
Like a wound besprent with salt,
And covered them with shaft and spear
As they fled consumed with fear.
All the leaders senseless fell,
Under Indrajit's black spell.
Flaming sword and flaming spear,
Smote the banars far and near.
A boon from Brahma he had used,
So Ram and Lakshman were abused,
And they allowed themselves to be
Pierced by his treachery.
To the ground they both did swoon
Because of Brahmadeva's boon.
Indrajit informed his sire
How the battle did transpire,
And told him how he did defeat
The Raghus, in his vain conceit.

74

Bibhishan assured them all
This was just a minor fall.
To honor Brahma they succumbed
Unto the weapon, and were numbed.
All the banars were subdued,
Their limbs upon the field were hewed.
Their mighty leaders there were found
Senseless on the bloody ground.
Of the heroes he could find
Jamwant had the clearest mind.
Jamwant did therein advise,
For Hanuman to cross the skies
And to the Himalayas fly
To where the healing herbs do lie.
Their fragrance would revive them all
And save them from this deathly pall.
Then Hanuman enlarged his size
And crushed the mountain with his thighs,
As he did prepare to leap
Across the vast and purple deep.
The earth and all of Lanka trembled,
Hanuman a hill resembled.
Roaring caused the faint of heart
To shiver, and their senses, part.
With a mighty bound he leapt,
And all around him then was swept
Into the air by rapid speed,
To save them with the herbs they need.
The orbit of the sun he trailed,
With the speed of wind he sailed,
Then Himavat before did loom
And Hanuman with hope did bloom.
He saw the dwellings of the sages,
And the herb that death assuages.
Ranging 'round that peak to find

The herbs for which he sought in kind,
But they did veil themselves from him,
Sinking just below the rim.
He tore the peak and flew away
Across the ocean and the spray.
Hanuman in brilliant light,
Outside of Lanka did alight.
The fragrance of the herbs soon healed
The warriors upon the field.
Those that had succumbed to death,
Now were healed and full of breath.
Then Hanuman returned that peak
To Himavat of great mystique.

75

The sun behind the mountains set
And Lanka was by fire beset.
That citadel of luxury,
That haven of debauchery,
Was attacked by banar men
Who beset its guardian.
From their drunken revelry,
The demons left their devilry,
And streamed into the city roads,
With their axes and their goads.
The gate was broken by a dart
Of Ram, where all the banars start,
And they besieged that august fort
With the rage they did transport.
Women and their children fanned
Into the streets, where they did stand,
As their houses raged with fire,
Symbolic of Prince Raghav's ire.
Palaces on fire did melt,
As rocks and trees the banars pelt
Flooding that belabored town

As banar men did tear it down.
The titan army followed course
To withstand that banar force,
And desperately a struggle passed
Where teeth and claws and weapons clashed.

76

Many foremost titans fought
And Angada, each one had sought,
Vanquishing each one in turn,
His anger did on each one burn.
The son of Kumbhakarn did fight,
Kumbha, who upholds the night,
And none of them could stand his might,
They all were vanquished in the fight.
But Sugriva challenged then,
Broke his bow, and rocks did spin.
Hand-to-hand the two did fight,
They were equal in their might.
They crushed each other with their blows,
Each intent to slay his foes.
Then finally that demon fell
Crashing through the gates of hell,
Succumbing to Sugriva's blow,
At last he did defeat his foe.

77

Kumbha's younger brother came,
Nikumbha, whom the titans claim.
None would dare approach that one
As his fiery mace was spun.
Hanuman did challenge then,
As his mace on him did spin,
But upon his chest it shattered,
Many were the fragments scattered.
Hand-to-hand the two did fight,

But none could match that banar's might,
And Hanuman tore off his head;
Nikumbha finally was dead.

78

Ravan was deranged with ire
To see his city set on fire.
Maharaksha he sent out
To Ram and Lakshman from there rout.
But evil portents did attend,
That demon would perceive his end.

79

A carnage did that demon cause
Slaying banars without pause,
But Prince Raghav challenged then,
And their battle did begin.
Shaft-to-shaft their arrows clashed
And to the earth their pieces crashed.
Then Prince Raghav broke the bow
Of that mighty demon foe.
Maharaksha drew his spear,
Emitting flames, as it did sear.
To Sri Ram the spear did wend,
But Ram did break it in the end.
With a dart he lanced his heart,
The life of him did soon depart.

80

Ravan called his foremost son
Who always had in battle won,
To sally forth and vanquish Ram
And victory derive therefrom.
So Indrajit invoked the fire
To satisfy his father's ire,
And Agni, thereby gratified

By the rites he glorified.
Auspicious omens did attend,
He would soon attain his end.
Invisible he did become
By the magic he did strum.
He rained his shafts upon the host,
But they could not discern his post.
Silent through the air he rode
And drove the banars with his goad.
Ram and Lakshman scoured the sky,
Endless shafts they sent to fly,
But none of them did hit the mark,
And fell to earth like strips of bark.
Ram and Lakshman wondered how
They could this titan disavow,
When from the field that demon left
Leaving many banars cleft.

81

Indrajit was full of wrath
Affected by the aftermath.
Once again he entered war
Intent to fight with them some more.
Perverse by nature, he was cruel,
Resorting to his magic tool.
An apparition did he form,
The role of Sita to perform,
Resembling her in each detail,
Upon his car with him would sail.
The banars saw her standing there,
In soiled dress and plaited hair,
Crying from his brutal blows,
He angered all his banar foes.
Indrajit announced to all,
To their terror and their pall,
He would slay Prince Raghav's wife,

Retaliating with her life.
And with his sword he pierced her breast,
Laughing at his bitter jest.
Now their battle was in vain,
Since Vaidehi had been slain.

82

But Hanuman regrouped his troop,
To flee from war they would not stoop.
And they assailed that titan force
Like a violent concourse.
A shower of both rocks and trees
They threw on Indrajit with ease.
The titans did retreat therein,
From brave and valiant banar men.
Then Indrajit again invoked
The God of Fire; the flames were stoked
And gratified; the fire's oblation
Was consumed through supplication.

83

Hanuman approached that one,
The House of Raghu's blessed son,
And told him that before their eyes
Sita met her cruel demise
At the hands of Ravan's son,
Vaidehi's life at last had run.
As clouds do veil the light of day,
Māyā did Prince Raghav sway.
Beset with grief, he lost his reason
Like a flower out of season.
Lakshman held him by his arm,
He who sheltered all from harm,
His burning tears did scorch his cheek,
He who could no longer speak.
Lakshman did lament in vain

That righteousness has now been slain,
And evil men attain the earth,
Obtaining wealth and righteous birth.
Dharma on the earth is dead
And evil is the brahmins' bread,
When death is chastity's reward,
Severed by a two-edged sword.

84

Bibhishan approached their midst
And ascertained the present gist.
But he assured the Best of Men
That Sita was alive within.
For Ravan did his consort guard,
None could enter in her yard.
That which Hanuman did see
Was false and quite illusory.
Indrajit by now had gone
To pour libations on that One
Who consumed his sacrifice,
And victory he did entice.
Lakshman now should break his rite
And challenge Indrajit to fight.

85

The Brahmasira weapon claimed,
Is how that titan now is famed.
If Indrajit completes his rite,
Then Ram is lost beneath its might.
But Brahmadeva did ordain
There was a way he could be slain.
Before he could complete his rite,
Challenge him in deadly fight.
So Lakshman and the army went,
So his rite they'd circumvent,

And defeat him in a duel
Before the fire had taken fuel.

86

Bibhishan did then advise
Lakshman with his counsel wise:
"The formation of the foe,
Quickly they should come to blow.
Destruction lies within this key,
To break their ranks ferociously,
Then Indrajit will have to rise,
Visible, before our eyes."
So the banars broke their rows
Defeating all their titan foes,
And Indrajit in wrath arose
Angered by their fierce blows.
Hanuman that one approached,
That banar who his anger broached.
And he did wound him with his dart,
Prepared to lance him through the heart
But Lakshman entered in the fray
And Indrajit was turned away.

87

Lakshman, also Bibhishan,
Saw the grove of Ravan's son,
And barred his way unto the tree
Where his sacrifice would be.
Lakshman challenged him to fight,
That awesome Ranger of the Night.
Indrajit unto them spoke,
The wrath within it did provoke:
"The brother of my father stands
Next to those from foreign lands,
Renouncing all his kith and kin
He injures them in hopes to win.

Perverse by nature must he be,
One who leaves his family."
Bibhishan replied in kind,
Expressing what was on his mind:
"A youthful prattle do I hear,
Laced with anger and with fear.
Cruel and wicked, and unjust,
A slave to every vice and lust,
A righteous man from such does flee
For doom becomes their destiny.
Slaughter of the saints and war
Is what in thee I do abhor.
Now thy end at last has come,
To Kakutstha you'll succumb."

88

Lakshman on the shoulders rode
On Hanuman as they did goad
The boasting of King Ravan's son,
Hence their battle had begun.
Their shafts did pierce and did strike
Each other with their pointed spike,
But none could get the upper hand,
For each his prowess did withstand.

89

A thousand shafts aloft did fly
Covering the clouds and sky
As both these warriors did fight,
Brandishing their strength and might.
Long this battle did go on,
But neither had the battle won.

90

The day turned into gloomy night
As still these warriors did fight.

Then Lakshman felled his driver dead
By cutting off his ghoulish head,
And Indrajit took up the rein
As arrows from them both did rain.
Then the banars killed his steed,
As they on the earth did bleed.
Then Indrajit jumped to the ground
And all the heavens did resound
With the twanging of their bows,
The banars and the banars' foes.

91

Then Indrajit returned inside
And on a chariot did ride
Back into the battle fray,
Turning all his foes away.
A savage struggle then ensued
As each the other was pursued
With celestial weapons, they
Caused the other one to stay.
By now his driver had been slain,
And his steeds pursued this vein,
As these heroes tensely fought,
The death of each the other sought.
Severely hurt, they would not stop,
Nor the battle would they drop.
Their weapons made the earth to shake,
And celestial devas quake.
The heavens burst in flames and flashed
As their magic weapons clashed.
Goaded now beyond return
The wrath of Lakshman rose to burn
And with a mantra-driven blow
He defeated Raghav's foe.
His shaft removed that demon's head
And Indrajit to earth fell dead.

The titan host did run away
Retreating from that fruitless fray,
And all the heavens showered flowers
Lauding Lakshman's hidden powers.
Devas were so gratified,
Exceedingly were satisfied.

92

Lakshman met his older brother
And they did embrace each other.
Learning that his foe was dead,
Raghav stroked his brother's head.
Raghav felt felicity
Seeing his humility.
Lakshman of his wounds was cured
By the herbs they had procured.
And everyone was satisfied
To have Prince Lakshman by their side.

93

When Ravan learned his son was dead
He swooned unto an earthen bed.
Long was he within that state
Where the mind and senses wait.
When he did recall his mind,
Still his loss and grief did find.
And then he was consumed with rage
For he could not his loss assuage.
His son who never knew defeat
Now the Lord of Death did greet.
Defeated by a mortal man,
Death at last fulfilled his plan.
Now he vowed to slay them both,
To cause their death he took an oath.
He raised his sword intent to slay
Vaidehi who had caused this fray.

But his counsellor prevented
Ravan's anger to be vented
On a woman here unarmed,
One who had not Ravan harmed.
So Ravan's wrath was circumvented,
To the Raghus it was vented.

94

Ravan did instruct his men
To return to fight again.
The titans and the banars fought,
The deaths of many there were brought,
And rivers of their blood would flow
Amongst the havoc they did sow.
Then Sri Ram approached the field,
A sacred weapon did he wield
Deluding all the titan host,
For they could not discern his post.
Everywhere the demons look
The face of Ram before them shook,
And titans did the titans slay,
Deluded in that bloody fray.
The titan army then was slain,
And Raghav did the battle gain.

95

The women of the titan men
Lamented long and hard within.
For Ram had laid their city waste
And massacred their men in haste.
For their menfolk they did long;
Their mourning was an evensong.

96

Ravan had resolved to fight,
Convinced he could the Raghus smite.

Mahodara, Mahaparshwa,
And the valiant Virupaksha
Went with him into the field,
Their prowess on the field to wield.
Ascending on his brilliant car,
Its luster could be seen from far.
But evil omens did attend
Those demons as they did intend
To fight Kakutstha and to win
A battle with the Best of Men.

97

The banars and the titans clashed,
Like two oceans they had crashed,
And rivers of their blood did flow,
As they were vanquished by their foe.
Virupaksha then did fight
Sugriva, full of fiery might.
But Virupaksha soon did fall
Beneath the sway of Yama's call
As Sugriva crushed his chest,
Forever laying him to rest.

98

Mahodara did accost
The banar army that was lost,
And as they fell beneath his blows,
They sought protection from their foes.
Sugriva did that one attend,
His strength and honor to defend,
And with a fatal, deadly blow
He vanquished his oppressive foe.

99

Mahaparshwa with his darts
Dismembered all the banars' parts,

And Angada approached him then
And fought alone intent to win.
Equally the two were cast
But Angada did win at last,
With a blow unto his chest,
His death did of his strength attest.

100

When Ravan saw his men were dead
He was seized by doubt and dread.
He foamed with anger and did rush
Preparing to Prince Raghav crush.
Lakshman had approached that one
But Ravan did Prince Lakshman shun.
To fight with Ram is what he sought,
He could vanquish him, he thought.
Many were the shafts pursued
That with magic were imbued.
With serpentine and donkey head
These apparitions caused one dread.
Lions, tigers, wolves, and bird,
Met those heroes undeterred,
And many were the darts that shone
Like the sun as they had flown.
Shafts of fire and water flew,
But neither could their foe subdue.

101

Weapons from the sea and sun,
All around the heavens spun.
Lakshman did his driver slay
And Bibhishan his horses flay.
Ravan was beset with anger,
Thrusting spears so fraught with danger
At his younger brother when
The brother of the Lord of Men

Did sever it a mighty dart;
Its fierceness could not impart.
In a transport of his rage,
Again a spear he did engage
For destruction of his brother,
Deadlier than was the other.
Lakshman stood before his friend
And shafts upon the king did wend,
Such that Ravan loosed the spear
On Lakshman, whom Ram held so dear.
A massive spear illumed with light
Did that mighty hero smite,
Passing through his broadened chest,
And half-way in the earth did rest.
To see his younger brother lay
Stricken in this battle fray,
Raghav was beset with grief
From this he could find no relief.
He pulled the spear and broke in half
That massive, deadly, magic staff.
Beset by Ravan's ruthless dart,
Raghav now in wrath did start,
And showered him with fiery snakes
Whose thirst for blood one never slakes.
Overwhelmed by Raghav's might
Ravan from the field took flight.

102

When Prince Raghav saw his brother,
He could see or hear no other
And of life could not rejoice,
Choked by tears and sobbing voice.
Of wives and friends there is no end,
But brothers one cannot expend.
He lost the meaning of his life
When Ravan caused his brother strife.

Blinded by his scorching tear,
The death of Lakshman did he fear.
But Sushena to him said
That his brother was not dead,
And Hanuman he sent to find
Herbs that would the spell unwind.
On Mahodaya Mountain are
Herbs that can this augur mar.
So Hanuman did bring it there;
That mountain did he lightly bear.
Sushena did prepare the herb
And the magic spell did curb.
Lakshman rose onto his feet,
Raghav in his arms did greet
His brother, who from death did turn;
His anguish now did cease to burn.
But Lakshman did his brother chide
For letting anguish there abide,
His vow should always be fulfilled
Regardless what the fates instilled.

103

Ram and Ravan then resumed;
Each was by his wrath consumed,
And desperately each one did fight
But they could not the other smite.
Ravan on his car did turn,
And Raghav did his arrows spurn,
But this arrangement was not fair,
With Ram on foot and him in air.
So Indra did his car bestow
So Ram could battle with his foe
With his driver and his steed,
Equipped with weapons he would need.
Their arrows on each other hailed
But neither one of them prevailed.

A myriad of serpents fell
From Ravan's black and deadly spell.
With tongues of flames these darts did seek
To pierce Ram and venom leak.
But from his bow Sri Ram did send
Eagles soaring in the wind
And they devoured every snake,
And Ravan in his wrath did quake.
Ravan did assail his foe,
Filling all the worlds with woe.
The sun grew dark and ocean sprayed
And all the devas were afraid
For Ram could not return the dart
That Ravan did on him impart.
As volcanoes do erupt
The wrath of Raghav was abrupt,
And the earth in terror swayed,
Perversely were the omens laid.
Like dissolution of the world,
Their weapons on each other hurled.

104

The sun by arrows was obscured
From the shafts that each had poured.
Ravan did the war fatigue;
Fighting now beyond his league.
And Raghav did belittle him,
For the evil of his whim,
Abducting Sita from the wood
When her protector from her stood.
To steal a woman made him great,
That kind of courage did he rate,
But now the wrath of Ram is faced,
The noose of death was round him placed.
Ravan fainted in his car;
His death did wait for him, not far.

His driver took him from the field
When he saw that he did yield.

105

Ravan did regain his sense
And wondered how he came there hence.
His anger on his tongue did lash
His driver, for this act so rash.
He was not a coward to
Retreat before he did subdue
His foe, and now his glory's lost,
At his driver's folly's cost.
But his driver did assure
His master, that his motive's pure.
To offer rest unto the steed
And master, at his time of need,
Is why he did withdraw from there,
Not his master to impair.
Satisfied, the king did heed
His driver and to war proceed.

106

Awaiting Ravan to return,
Ram was also tired in turn.
The sage Agastya did appear
To impart the prayer most dear
By which the foe he then defeats,
A hymn where one the sun entreats:
"Oh brilliant orb within the sky,
My soul and breath to thee do fly.
Thou art the refuge of my speech,
Attainable, within my reach.
Thou art the slayer of my foes,
The vanquisher of all my woes,
Thy light illumines all my sin,
A fortress do I find within.

All illness and disease do fly,
When upon thee I rely.
All weakness and fatigue are gone,
When I discern the brilliant sun.
You nourish me and give me rest,
Thy beauty and thy grace attest.
In thy presence I do feel
All my wounds and sorrows heal.
Thou art the source from which I come
And return when I succumb.
My fears and worries fly away
When I am brought beneath thy sway.
Eternally thy name is *Om*,
Where the Vedas find their home.
A thousand rays from thee proceed
To satisfy my every need.
Thou dost my life and breath sustain,
Nourishment from thee I gain.
Thou art the refuge of the wise,
Fearlessly, thy love does guise.
Salutations do I bring
To that from which my life does spring.
Salutations do I give
To that which makes my soul to live.
Salutations do I leave
To that which stops my soul to breathe,
And salutations to that flame,
Where death no longer can one claim.
May auspiciousness attend
The one who knows thee as thy friend.
Eternally, thy light does shine,
Thy nature is to all divine."
Thus, Agastya did so teach
Raghav this auspicious speech,
And in his need it would not fail,
That good fortune would prevail.

Then to Raghav He appeared,
The sun, whom all the saints revered,
And Ram was fortified within,
He who was the Best of Men.

107

Ravan stood prepared to fight
But evil omens came to light
Predicting Ravan's swift defeat
And victory to Ram, so sweet.
Their chariots in circles turned
As each one, full of ire, had burned.
And many were the shafts that flew
Creating an unearthly hue.

108

That awesome Ranger of the Night
Entered once again the fight,
But Ravan failed to hit his mark,
Uselessly his shafts did spark.
But Raghav's arrows did not fail
To hit their mark and on him hail.
He broke his banner, shot his steed,
And circled round with endless speed.
The banars and the titans stopped
Their fighting, and their weapons dropped,
Witnessing that strangest fray
Which Ram and Ravan did array.

109

For seven days and every night
The two without a pause did fight.
Steed to steed they each did stand,
And on their steeds their shafts did land.
Each was wounded and did bleed,
But these shafts they did not heed.

Raghav was consumed with ire
And in the battle did not tire.
The head of Ravan did he sever,
But that demon, who was clever,
Grew again another one
Another one from there he spun.
Many were the heads he cut
But Ravan he could not obstruct,
And Raghav pondered deep within,
How he could this battle win.

110

Raghav's driver to him spoke,
The dart of Brahma to invoke
And vanquish him whose time had come,
Now to fate he would succumb.
So Ram recalled that awesome dart,
Annihilation as its heart;
Hissing like an angry snake,
Death alone that fire could slake.
On Ravan did that weapon fall,
And Yama with his noose did call
As Ravan lay without his breath,
Finally succumbed to death.
The titan army cried their tears,
Now consumed with hopeless fears.

111

Now his brother's gone to death,
Deprived of all his vital breath,
And Bibhishan had felt his loss,
Upon the tide of grief to toss.
For courage and for prowess famed,
Ravan was for valor named.
Bibhishan intensely felt
The loss that destiny had dealt.

112

The consorts of that titan king,
Widowhood on them did spring.
Rolling in the dust, they cried,
When they learned their lord had died.
The call of destiny is first;
Birth and death, it has dispersed.

113

Mandodari, Ravan's queen,
Saw the reason yet unseen,
That Ram was the Eternal Soul,
And Ravan had now paid the toll.
He who had subdued his sense,
They in turn did him dispense.
All her family now was lost,
Ravan's lust their lives had cost.
Now they would begin the rite
To honor him, whom Ram did smite.
But Bibhishan refused to go
And honor him, who was his foe.
But Raghav to his friend did claim
That death alone does douse the flame
Of enmity that did exist
But in the realms of death desist.
So Bibhishan performed the rites
For that Ranger of the Night,
Who long was known as Lanka's Best,
Now his soul was laid to rest.

114

The chariot that Indra sent,
Its usefulness that now was spent,
Was dismissed and thus returned,
Now that Ravan had been spurned.
Bibhishan Ram did install,

He would rule the titans all,
As the King of Lanka, he
Rejoiced with great felicity.
Raghunanda then did send
Hanuman, his timeless friend,
To bear his greeting to that one
That Ravan did to death succumb,
And ask his consort of her mind,
What happiness she now could find.

115

Hanuman found Janaki
Beneath the same Ashoka tree.
Forlorn, besmeared, and streaked with tears,
Janaki, her sorrow sears.
At first she did not know his face
And then delight did take its place.
Joyously she met her son
As tears between them both did run.
Hanuman did then explain
That Ravan was by Raghav slain.
Raghav now did wait to see
His consort, dearest Maithili.
Her happiness deprived her speech;
Now that chasm she could breach.
She desired to see her lord,
Now the tide of grief could ford.
Hanuman did want to slay
The titans that kept her at bay,
But Janaki to him replied,
To slay them would not good betide.
Obedient unto their king,
They only did his orders bring.
His honor it would not enhance
To slay them in this circumstance.

To see her lord was her desire,
Her love did scorch her like a fire.

116

Hanuman relayed the word
That Sita had on him conferred.
Joy and sorrow marked their place
Across the sea of Raghav's face.
He closed his eyes and shed a tear,
And Bibhishan was by him near.
He bade that king to greet his wife
She who now was freed from strife,
And offer her celestial gems,
Costly robes and golden hems,
And after she had bathed to dress,
And had washed her silken tress,
To bring Vaidehi back again,
Thus did speak the Best of Men.
Bibhishan approached that one
So mournful like a fallen sun.
Respectfully he bowed his head,
Repeating words that Ram had said.
But Sita did request to see
Her lord as she appeared to be.
Bibhishan did then convey,
She should Raghav's wish obey.
Then Maithili, who jewels adorn,
In a palanquin was borne
Before the banars and her lord,
The one whom Raghu had adored.
Bibhishan did make a space
For Maithili her lord to face,
But Ram commanded him to cease,
That with the banars to keep peace.
She whom eyes had never seen,
She who was Prince Raghav's queen,

Before that army was exposed;
Confusion in her mind had posed.
Bibhishan and Lakshman felt
Remorse for this which Ram had dealt.
When the eyes of Sita fell
On Ram, her grief did then dispel.
Like a lotus full in bloom,
The love of Ram did her consume.

117

When Ram beheld his lovely wife,
His heart was riven by a knife:
"Oh princess born with faultless limbs,
We avenged these evil whims.
Lakshman and great Hanuman,
Sugriva and King Bibhishan,
Together did we win the fight,
And thy abductor did we smite.
The blight upon my name is gone,
Since the battle we had won.
Born into my father's house,
I avenged my wounded spouse.
The southern region is reclaimed,
That which was for terror famed.
Not for thee alone I fought,
Protection of the saints I sought.
Yet a question has remained,
Thy conduct, while you were detained.
The people are confused with doubt,
They wonder if you were devout.
I give thee leave to go from here,
For I cannot abide thee near.
Thy presence causes pain to me,
Now go and seek thy destiny.
Bharat, Lakshman, Hanuman,
Sugriva or King Bibhishan—

Choose amongst them, thou art free,
No longer can you live with me.
For staying in that titan's house,
Who lusted for thee as his spouse,
You cannot now with me return,
As my wife I do thee spurn."
Bitterly Vaidehi wept;
The valley of despair was swept.

118

Raghunanda stood like death,
Piercing words upon his breath.
And Sita to her lord replied,
As she stood next to his side:
"You speak just like a common man,
Given to a common plan,
And cherish not the hand I gave
When love did bind me as your slave.
Of the earth this body's born,
Of chastity I am not shorn.
By my will, I touched no man,
These events the fates did plan.
Defenseless, one did dare to grasp
This body, like a writhing asp.
But my heart to thee was true,
None other did I e'er pursue.
When Hanuman I first did meet,
You should have told this vain conceit,
And then I would have dropped this life
As thy poor, mistreated wife,
And spared thee all this futile war,
For one whom thou dost love no more.
Since my faithfulness you doubt,
I, whose conduct was devout,
Today will enter in the fire,
Lakshman, now prepare the pyre!"

No one dared to change the mood,
For Raghav did like Yama brood.
Reluctantly he made the pyre,
Burning with a brilliant fire,
And Maithili did circle round
Her lord who was by honor bound.
Janaki, the fire invoked,
Her purity was then evoked.
If her heart to Ram was true,
Then sanctity would be her due.
And fearlessly she met the flame
And all the women cried her name,
And titans and the banars cried
To see her in the fire abide.

119

Raghav rigidly stood near
From his eye did fall a tear.
The devas in the sky appeared
And that hero they revered.
Then the gods did ask of him,
Why he spoke like this to them,
When he was that cosmic source,
That all-pervading, living force?
Ram did think he was a man
Unaware of Brahma's plan,
And bade Swayambhu to recall
His history, to tell him all.
Brahmadeva did reply
From where he was within the sky
That Raghu was an avatar,
An eternal, guiding star.
Narayan was his honored name,
Ram, Narayan were the same.
He was Vishnu and the Boar,
Vāmana, and many more.

He took a human birth to kill
Ravan with his martial skill.
Sita, Lakshmi, are the same,
They are known by either name.

120

The God of Fire to Ram appeared
With Maithili, who was not seared,
And said her innocence was pure,
Her love for Ram made her secure.
Neither by her thought or deed,
Did her love of Ram secede.
Never should she be reproached,
For Ravan had not her encroached.
Raghunanda said he knew
That Sita in her love was true,
But for the sake of common men,
He wanted them to see again.
Without his wife he could not live
For she to him his breath did give.
Reunited they did stand,
Victorious upon the land.

121

Shiva did to Raghav speak,
Shrouded in His own mystique.
To Ayodhya he should turn,
To his mothers there return,
And consolation he should give,
Bharat he should now forgive.
Then Dasharatha did appear
Descending from his lofty sphere,
And spoke unto his dearest son
Whose destiny the devas spun.
Raghav did to all avow
To fulfill his father's vow,

And Dasharatha was redeemed
By the acts that Ram esteemed.
He blessed his sons and Janaki
And felt supreme felicity.

122

Then Devendra to him spoke,
A boon he wanted to invoke.
So Ramachandra asked him then
To return to life again
The banars that for Ram had died,
Healed of wounds and sanctified,
Full of vigor they should be
Alive with great vitality.
The banars did the god restore,
Complete as they had been before.

123

Ram did have a strong desire
In accordance with his sire,
To Ayodhya now return,
And greet his mothers all in turn.
Bibhishan did him invite,
To stay at Lanka for the night,
But Prince Raghav would not stay;
He wanted to be on his way.
Pushpak was the famous car
That Ravan stole from lands afar,
Like a palace in the air
With the speed of thought so rare.
And they ascended in that car
To take them over lands afar,
So in a day they could return
To home, to be where they did yearn.

124

Raghav now prepared to go
And Bibhishan did ask to know
What he now should plan to do;
What is the course he should pursue?
All the banars should receive
Wealth and jewels before they leave,
So Prince Raghav did advise
That titan who was kind and wise.
All the banars satisfied,
Raghav did ascend to ride.
They desired to see him be
Installed with wealth and luxury
As Koshala's newest king,
This the wish that they did bring.
And Prince Raghav did agree
That they could accompany
The chariot, and with him fly
Across the land where home did lie.

125

As they through the sky did course,
Raghav spun a mild discourse
Describing to his consort's ear
The names of places far and near.
When Kishkindha they could see,
Vaidehi asked him pleasingly,
If their wives could come with them
For everyone did cherish him.
So they stopped the car and there
All the consorts did repair
To the car as they did spin
Through the air to home again.

126

Then Raghav reached the hermitage
Surrounded by thick foliage
Of the sage who gave them rest
And by his presence they were blest.
Bharadwaja had foreseen
His journey and with love was keen.
And by his penance he did see
All events with clarity.
Whatever did Sri Ram befall,
Bharadwaja could recall.
And to Ram he gave a boon
That all the trees would blossom soon
Laden with celestial fruit
For the banars' sweet pursuit.

127

Ayodhya now to Ram was near
As all approached it with good cheer,
And Hanuman he sent about
As his minister and scout
To approach his younger brother;
Now they would find one another.
Hanuman, in human guise,
Found Prince Bharat in this wise.
Penitent, he had grown worn,
For Ram's misfortune did he mourn.
And Hanuman approached that one,
Brilliant like the ranging sun,
That Prince Raghav had come near
And he should now be of good cheer.
Bharat brightened like the moon
And gave to Hanuman a boon
For bringing to his ears the news,
Beatitude did him suffuse.

128

In great detail that banar told
The feats that Ram attained so bold,
And all that did those three befall,
The good and bad, he told it all.
Like a man reborn anew,
The story did new life imbue.
Bharat listened to the word
That bliss and happiness conferred.
On the morrow he would greet
Raghav whom he longed to meet.

129

All the townsfolk did rejoice
Chanting praises as one voice.
Streets and house they did adorn
Like a bride who was reborn.
All the citizens assembled,
Full-blown lotuses resembled,
Waiting for their absent king
And all the love that he would bring.
Finally the car did land
At the place where they had planned.
Bharat in respect bowed low,
With humbleness his face did glow.
And Raghav clasped him to his heart,
For long the two had been apart.
And on his feet he placed the shoe
That ruled the land in Raghav's lieu.
And returned the kingdom to
Raghunanda who was true.
All the profits did increase
Ten-fold in this time of peace.
And Ram and Bharat were content
That now his time without was spent.
To Kaushalya Ram did bow,

He who did fulfil his vow,
And happiness her heart instilled,
Contentment now her soul had filled.
Ram in turn did greet each queen,
Finally, their hearts serene.
The titans and the banars cheered
To see Ayodhya they revered,
And everyone was filled with love,
Like gentle mist from God above.

130

Vashishtha and each minister,
Did the rites administer.
The coronation was complete
And Ram in splendor was replete.
In charity he knew no bound,
In jewels and wealth, his guests were found.
And kine and gold he gave therein,
The twice-born known as brahmin men.
As king that prince was now installed,
And happiness upon them called.
The banars and the titans turned
And to their kingdoms they returned.
Ram and Sita reigned in bliss,
Their happiness did now egress.
Felicity did there abound;
Blissfulness was all around.
All their wounds were washed away
When Ram returned to live and stay.
This epic tale Valmiki wrote,
This story does great faith emote.
Those who listen to this tale,
Over obstacles prevail.
Any wish one does desire,
By this tale, it does transpire.
This epic in entirety

Leads one to security.
Prosperity becomes the friend
Of him who listens to the end.
Great benefits one does accrue
When he hears this epic through.

Uttara Kāṇḍa

UTTARA KĀṆḌA is the last section of the *Ramayana*, the description of Rama's life after his return from fourteen years of exile. Rama and Sita enjoy supreme felicity, and Sita conceives. Rama learns that the people of Ayodhya condemn him for receiving his wife after she has lived in another man's house. Rama commands Lakshman to take Sita to the hermitage of Valmiki, who adopts Sita as his spiritual daughter and gives her his protection. Sita gives birth to twin boys, Kush and Lav. Twelve years later Rama begins the ashwamedha ceremony. Kush and Lav recite the *Ramayana* in the streets of Ayodhya as well as at Rama's palace. Rama asks the sage Valmiki to bring Sita to court to publicly take an oath proving her purity. Mother Earth opens, and Sita descends into the earth. Rama is beset with grief. Yama comes disguised as a brahmin to speak to Rama in private, provided no one disturbs them under penalty of death. Lakshman interrupts while Yama and Rama are conversing, and thus leaves his body.

Uttara Kāṇḍa

1

Established in his kingdom now,
Raghav who fulfilled his vow,
Enjoyed supreme felicity,
In splendor and simplicity.
The foremost of the sages came
To extol King Raghav's name,
For now the world was purged of those
Demons known as munis' foes.
Of all the titans he did kill,
Indrajit required great skill.
Raghav sought from them to know
Why they did regard this foe.

2

The story now to Ram they told,
Going back to times of old,
Recounting now the parentage
Of Ravan's ancient lineage.
Prajapati did have a son
Resplendent like a searing sun.
Disciplined and virtuous,
His tapas was quite arduous.
A paramrishi did they call

Pulastya, so beloved of all.
On Mount Meru did he sit
Engaged in tapas as was fit.
At his pleasant hermitage,
Amid the fragrant foliage,
Innocently girls did play
Where that rishi chose to stay.
Irritated by the girl
A curse upon her did he hurl,
That who should fall beneath his glance
Would conceive, as if by chance.
All the girls did run away
Afraid of what the sage did say.
One rishi's daughter there did stray
Who did not hear what he did say,
And instantly she did conceive
Though she could not this believe.
To her father she returned
Who asked her how her womb had burned,
And she replied she did not know,
But the truth to him did show.
He took his daughter to the sage
As an offering to gage
His daughter to that pious saint,
She who was without a taint.
By her conduct he was pleased,
Her character had him appeased.
He blessed her son that grew within
For righteousness among all men.
Vishrava became his name;
For piety he gathered fame.

                        3
Vishrava just like his sire,
Was resplendent like the fire.
Bharadwaja gave the hand

Of his daughter as he planned.
She gave birth unto a son
And virtue through his veins was spun.
Vaishravana became his name,
The Guardian of Wealth the same.
A thousand ages passed as one,
In tapas all his time was run.
Brahmadeva then appeared
To him who made himself endeared.
The Lord of Wealth he did become,
The guardian of all its sum.
Pushpak had the sage received,
A boon from Brahma he achieved.
Vaishravana addressed his sire
Where he should to now retire.
A citadel upon a hill
Remained abandoned, by god's will.
Vishvakarma did construct
This city did his sire instruct.
Vaishravana should there repair;
To settle there he should prepare.
That saintly one became their king
And righteousness and wealth did bring.

4

Raghav of the sages asked,
Of the rakshasas long past:
What was their true origin,
They who were the foes of men?
First the waters were created,
Then the creatures procreated,
Then they asked God what to do;
They had thirst and hunger, too.
Rakshasas were the protectors
Yakshas were the sacrificers.
A rakshasa of fierce might,

And one born with divine insight,
Came upon the gracious earth,
There they did obtain their birth.
The ascetic was Praheti,
And the frightful one was Heti.
Praheti sought the solitude,
But Heti had a wife pursued.
Vidyutkesha was his son,
Having splendor like the sun.
Sālakaṭankaṭā he wed
That rakshasa whom all did dread.
On a mountain she gave birth,
Then left her son upon the earth.
Shiva and Parvati found
The crying baby on the ground.
In compassion Shiva gave
Immortality to save
The baby and enhanced his age
To match his mother's at this stage.
A celestial car was given,
Through the heavens he had driven.
Through Parvati's saving grace,
She blessed the whole rakshasa race
That babies born would have the age
Equal to their mother's stage.
And the women when conceived
Instantly would be relieved.
Sukesha was the baby's name,
And through Lord Hara gathered fame.

5

Sukesha was quite blest in life,
A gandharvi was his wife.
Three great sons were born to them,
But earth was subject to their whim.
Malyavan had brothers two,

Mali and Sumali, too.
A course of penance they did take,
And by their tapas they did shake
The heavens with their churning fire
To bring them to the heaven's sire.
Brahmadeva did approach
Those rakshasas who fire did broach.
Many boons he did bestow,
Invincible unto their foe,
They would have longevity,
Devoted unto each those three.
Arrogant, the three did roam
Like the world became their home.
Of Vishvakarma they did ask
A citadel to them unmask,
Equivalent unto the gods
Where they could live, those demi-gods.
Lanka had by him been built,
In gold the palaces were gilt.
All the rakshasas could dwell
Within that fortress very well.
Three gandharvis then did wed
Those brothers whom the gods did dread.
Many sons to them were born,
But all the sages were forlorn,
For all their rites they did impede,
They did a protector need.

6

In unison the gods did ask
Lord Shiva to take up their task,
Vanquishing Sukesha's son
Who from their kingdom made them run.
But Hara to the gods replied,
That he would not their battle ride.
To Hari they should now approach,

He would those rakshasas broach.
So He who did uphold the mace
All the devas turned to face,
And they asked that Golden One
To reclaim what they did shun.
Vishnu did agree to fight,
And promised all their foes to smite.
The brothers heard what they had planned,
And so decided then to land
In devaloka and to fight
With Vishnu, with their joined might.
So those Rangers of the Night
Did before the Lord alight.

7

Narayan did the demons rout,
In terror they did turn about.
His shining disc did cut the head
Of Mali, leaving that one dead.
To Lanka all the demons fled,
But death upon those foes had tread.

8

Narayan made the demons dwell
In Rasātala, nether hell.
Vaishravana did there abide
In Lanka they did all reside.
Ram is that illumined soul
Whose virtue sages all extol.
Narayan, Ram, they are the same,
Known to us by either name.
That is how Ram came to slay
Those demons in that awesome fray.
Whenever righteousness declines,
Upon the earth the Lord inclines.

9

Sumali from his hell did rear
And found the Lord of Wealth was near.
Kaikasi was his daughter born,
Fragile like the pristine morn.
To Vaishrava she was sent
With marriage as her sire's intent.
At the hour known as dusk,
Like a doe drawn to the musk,
She approached that brilliant sage
Who in tapas did engage.
Because of the ungodly hour,
Evil children of dark power,
Would unto that girl be born,
Kaikasi then became forlorn.
But the child born to her last
Would in righteousness be cast.
Dashanana the eldest son,
Then Kumbhakarn on earth was spun,
To Shurpanakha she next gave birth,
And Bibhishan then graced the earth;
Dashanana and younger brother
Were the scourge of every other.
Tapas by them was pursued,
Their senses by them were subdued.

10

Ten thousand years did quickly fly
As Bibhishan did purify
His tapas that was now complete,
Was to Brahmadeva sweet.
Boons the Grandsire had conferred
On him, where righteousness concurred.
Always fixed upon his duty,
Virtue found its full-blown beauty.
Immortality was given

To the one who's duty-driven.
Dashanana did too perform
Austerity of rigid form,
As every thousand years he cut
A head in rites he did conduct.
Nine thousand years did pass this way
And on the tenth as he did pray,
Brahmadeva had appeared,
That demon had the Lord revered.
Immortality is what
Dashanana from Him had sought.
But this the Grandsire would not give,
Like other men he had to live.
Invincible unto his foes,
Dashanana too quickly chose,
But of man he failed to name,
Death will visit him the same.
His heads that were consumed with fire
Returned from that auspicious pyre.
Of Kumbhakarn they were afraid,
The gods then Brahma did persuade
To bemuse him ere he speak
Refuge did they humbly seek.
Saraswati veiled his speech
So his ambitions could not reach.
And when he asked to grant him boons,
He asked to sleep for many moons.
And Brahmadeva did so grant
The wishes that the gods did plant.

11

Sumali to the surface came,
And all the demons did the same.
Fearless now by Ravan's grace
They wanted to reclaim their place.
In Lanka they did want to live,

And asked Dhanada them to give.
Vaishravana did leave that place
And to Kailasha turned his face.
There he did a city build,
With artisans and craftsmen skilled.
In beauty it was unsurpassed,
In luxury their days had passed.
Ravan did the fort invade,
And as the King of Titans stayed.

12

Shurpanakha in time was wed,
And her brothers in their stead.
The wife of Ravan had a son,
An awesome strength through him did run.
Meghanad became his name,
As Indrajit we him acclaim.

13

Kumbhakarn to sleep succumbed,
For thousand years he was benumbed.
And Ravan did the heavens shake,
And rishis in their fear did quake.
Vaishravana again subdued
His mind by penance he pursued.
His left eye that beheld the sight
Of Uma, blinded in the light.
Hara did the sage befriend
When his tapas there did end.
When he returned he heard the news
How Ravan did the worlds abuse.
In honor of his father's name,
He thought he could his brother tame,
And sent a messenger to say
His abuses should now stay.

But Ravan did set out to fight;
He sought his brother then to smite.

14

Ravan had a thirst for war;
To fight his brother he then swore.
With the rakshasas he went,
To fight with Dhanada intent.
The mighty rakshasas did fight,
And all the yakshas did he smite.
Vanquished, many of them dead,
In all directions they had fled.

15

Then the two alone did stand
With many weapons in their hand.
A deadly battle did effuse
And Ravan had recourse to ruse,
And changed his form amid the fray
Attempting to his brother slay.
Finally he did defeat
Dhanada, forced to retreat.
The munis bore him far away,
Where he could in safety stay.
Pushpak, that celestial car,
Was by Ravan taken far.

16

Dashanana above did sail,
Across the world he did travail.
Then suddenly the car did halt
As if someone did him assault.
A fearful dwarf did then appear;
Black and stout, he was severe.
Nandi to that demon said,
He could not this mountain tread.

Shiva and Parvati played
Upon this mountain where they stayed.
None could enter here this mount,
Dashanana did this discount.
He laughed at Nandi's monkey face;
A curse on him did Nandi place,
As banars, gods would soon be born,
Dashanana he did forewarn.
Dashanana chose to uproot
That mountain like a savage brute.
But Maheshwara with his toe,
Pressed it down upon his foe.
Dashanana then loudly cried
For he could not the pain abide,
And for a thousand years it stayed,
And to Lord Shiva he had prayed.
Bhava was appeased at last,
And a boon to him did cast,
That Ravan would become his name
For his cry that gave him fame,
And long would be his life in years
To move about, and lacking fears.
Ravan like a mongrel fought,
To vanquish anyone he sought.

17

Wearing bark and shearling skin,
A female virgin without sin,
Was seen by Ravan as he passed
The mountain where her hut was cast.
Smitten by the God of Love,
He sought her as his ladylove.
In penance was she then engaged,
For love of Vishnu she was gaged.
Vedavati was her name,
Dashanana by lust inflamed,

Grabbed and pulled her matted hair
But she did cut it off right there.
Desecrated by his touch
She would not abide his clutch.
She ascended into fire,
And cursed him from the sacred pyre
That she would cause his mortal death,
These the last words on her breath.
As Sita she is to us known,
The means of Ravan's death was shown.
And Ram is that exalted Soul,
The Puroshottam we extol.

18

As Ravan traveled on his way,
A sacrifice was underway.
There he did that rite obstruct,
That King Marutta did construct.
The devas that were in the rite
Were seized by terror and by fright.
The shapes of many beasts they took,
Hoping they could Ravan rook.
All the rishis Ravan ate,
Thus his hunger could he sate.
When he left the devas blest
These animals that gave them rest.
The swan, chameleon, and the crow,
And peacock, do their blessings show.

19

Always searching for a fight,
In war he found a great delight.
To submit or fight he said,
To fight with him they would be dead.
And so the kings of men desist
From fighting, as he would insist.

Then to Ayodhya Ravan came,
And to the king he said the same.
But Anaranya did him fight,
And Ravan did his army smite.
And as that mighty king then fell
A curse on Ravan did he spell,
That in his race would be one born
Forever in his side a thorn.
And he would cause that titan's death,
Those the last words on his breath.

20

Over earth that titan ranged
And all inhabitants estranged.
Then Narad did that titan meet,
Who paid obeisance at his feet.
And Narad asked him why to sow
Terror on this mortal foe?
Death he should now overcome,
Yama to him should succumb.
To Rasātala Ravan went,
To vanquish Yama quite intent.

21

Narad quickly beat him there
To see how Yama then would fare.
Vaivasvat did greet that sage
Who welfare of the worlds did gage.
He was meting just rewards
To souls who came into his wards.
His army did those regions guard,
They were awesome and were hard.
There were those cast into hells,
Filling it with cries and yells.
Some of them wild dogs did eat,
Yet their flesh would not deplete,

And burning sand did line the shore
Of bloody rivers filled with gore.
Some were tortured by their thirst
And hunger, while their bellies burst.
Thousands of those souls were there
Who in life would never share.
And others opulently dwelt,
Receiving what their karmas dealt,
Surrounded by celestial girls,
With gold and gems and milky pearls.
Then Ravan on his car came there
Illumining that darkened lair,
Releasing evil souls from hell
Who in punishment did dwell.
Yama's army did pursue
That monarch and his car did hew.
Divine in nature, Pushpak could
Renew itself just where it stood.
Countless soldiers fought with him
But easily he vanquished them.
Overcome by ruthless foes,
Belabored by their endless blows,
He did pashupata choose,
And loosed that awesome, sacred ruse.
A fire upon them all did stray
Consuming that audacious fray.

22

Death and Ravan then did fight
For seven days and every night,
Agitating all the world,
By the weapons that they hurled.
Like Kala at the end of time
Their battle was a paradigm.
Yama raised his rod of death,
To snatch away that titan's breath,

But Brahma to them both appeared,
The boon he gave must be adhered.
So Yama disappeared from sight,
Forfeiting that Ranger's fight.

23

Ravan in his pride assailed
Many races as he sailed.
To Varuna's court he went,
Engaged in war his time was spent.
He defeated every son,
That battle in the waters won.
But Varuna was away
To hear divine musicians play.

24

Many women did he take,
His awful lust he could not slake.
The daughters of great kings and gods
Were captured by his evil rods.
Their consorts and their kin did kill,
He took them all against their will.
Condemnation did not count
To Ravan who was tantamount.
These women who were chaste at heart,
Did a curse on him impart.
Through a woman he would fall,
The cause of death to him would call.
Ravan with his car had flown
Back to his bejeweled throne.
Shurpanakha did him accost,
Who because of him was lost.
Ravan had her husband slain,
Shurpanakha did cry in vain.
To Janasthan he sent his crew,
The forest there they would subdue.

Shurpanakha and Khara went
To Daṇḍaka, where they were sent.

25

At the Nikumbhila grove
Meghanad his magic wove.
Many rites he there performed,
The devas to his wish conformed.
In silence was his ritual,
His silence was habitual,
So when his sire approached his son,
The family priest did greet that one.
Bibhishan addressed that king,
Whom many women he did bring;
Their cousin had been swept away
When a demon there did stray.
Her brothers were not in the house,
So he took her for his spouse.
This was the karma he accrued
For these acts that others rued.
So Ravan did prepare to fight
That one who did his ire ignite.
Madhu was that titan named;
For his valor he was famed.
Ravan saw that demon's lair
And found his cousin waiting there.
She did supplicate her king
Not to there his anger bring.
And Madhu would become his friend,
His kingdom and his life defend.
So in friendship they did go
To fight with their eternal foe.
At Kailasha they had camped
The army, at the base encamped.

26

On Kailasha they did stay,
The army under sleep did sway.
The full moon did ascend the sky
As Ravan, in its beams did lie.
The forest trees together bloomed
And gentle birds each other groomed.
Essences upon the wind
Gaily did their fragrance send,
Celestial nymphs did laugh and dance
Indulging in a light romance.
Ravan was with lust aflame,
His reason lost; his senses lame.
Seen by Ravan on the crest
Was Rambha, she of ample breast.
Besmeared with paste and flowered hair,
Adorned with jewels and garlands fair,
With shapely hips and tapered thighs,
She fanned the fire of Ravan's eyes.
He stopped her course as she had passed
And 'neath his gaze, she was aghast.
He asked her where she went this night
Beneath the stars in full moonlight,
And who would stroke her breast and hips,
And who would taste her salty lips?
Prostrate at his feet she lay,
And for his mercy she did pray.
She was like his daughter now,
Her love she did his son avow.
Nalakuvara, the son
Of that great Exalted One,
Vaishravana his older brother;
They're related to each other.
Ravan to her did reply,
These rules to her did not apply.
That devas have so many wives

A nymph with many lovers thrives.
So he took her by his force,
Ignorant of fate's new course.
Like a trampled flower, she
Was violated ruthlessly.
Like the brilliant morning sun
Was Vaishravana's pure son.
She prostrated at his feet
And his pardon did entreat,
That Ravan did give her assault
Though with her there was no fault.
And the rishi saw the truth,
And knew what she had said was sooth.
On Ravan did he lay a curse
For this act which was perverse,
That if he did a woman take,
Against her will his lust to slake,
In seven pieces would it fall,
His head would break and death would call.
And joy in the heavens showered,
For that sage's words empowered.

27

Ravan with his infantry,
His army and his cavalry
To devaloka did ascend;
The heavens with their roars did rend.
A mighty battle did ensue,
As each the other did pursue.
Sumali was in battle killed
By Savitra, who there did wield
A mace upon his demon head,
And struck that mighty titan dead.

28

The son of Indra then did fight
The son of Ravan with his might.
Then Ravan, Indra there did stand
In opposition on that land
And shafts did darken up the sky
As thousands of those darts did fly.

29

The army of the demons slain,
Ravan in his wrath did rain
Shafts on the celestial host,
Coursing through their outer post.
Indrajit the gods pursued;
Invisible, his magic used.
He bound Devendra with his rope
And all the devas gave up hope.
In victory they left the field
With Indra who to them did yield.

30

Brahma had them all addressed
When Indra was by Ravan pressed.
By his prowess he was pleased
But wanted Indra then released.
What ransom could they give in turn
For Indra, whom they all did spurn?
Immortality is what
The son of Ravan from Him sought.
But this, the Grandsire would not grant,
Could something else his wish supplant?
So Meghanad addressed that One
From where the universe was spun,
That when he had adored the fire
Before he did to war transpire,
And did ascend upon his car

In preparation for the spar,
Then no one could him defeat,
That was the boon he did entreat.
Brahmadeva to him gave
The boon that Meghanad did crave.
And Indrajit would be his name,
Because he had subdued the same.
Gautam long ago did curse
Indra for an act perverse.
When he ravished Gautam's wife
That sage was filled with ire and rife
And cursed Devendra to be caught
In a battle that he fought.
So Indra then a rite pursued,
With his senses all subdued,
And reascended to his throne
And the kingdom he did own.

31

Once when Ravan ranged the sky
Searching for a foe to vie,
King Arjuna did he meet
In hopes he could that king defeat.
But from his palace he was gone.
Proceeding, Ravan came upon
The Narmada with fragrant shore,
Which lotuses and herons wore.
On that river he did gaze,
And of her beauty did he praise.
There they bathed and passed the time
In this pastoral pastime.

32

Suddenly the river rushed
And Ravan's offerings were crushed.
Arjuna in the river played,

And with his arms the water stayed.
He who was a thousand-armed,
Had his enemies alarmed.
Ravan challenged him to fight
After he his aides did smite.
And Arjuna quickly bound
That demon, on the barren ground.
Ravan had not that one harmed,
He who was a thousand-armed.
Arjuna to his palace went,
And Ravan was beside him pent.

33

He was by Arjuna jailed,
And all celestials cheered and hailed.
Then Pulastya came to know
That Ravan's captive by his foe.
Brilliant like a thousand rays,
Pulastya did illume the days
And where Arjuna ruled with fame,
The son of Brahma to there came.
Arjuna with a gladdened heart
Met that sage who lives impart.
By his presence he was blest,
And joyfully received his guest.
Pulastya did request the king
Since affection he did bring,
That Arjuna let him go,
He who was that monarch's foe.
In friendship now the two were wrought
And with each other never fought.

34

Ravan ranged the earth to fight,
He looked for anyone with might.
To Kishkindha did he come,

Hoping Bāli would succumb.
Bāli to the sea had gone,
And Ravan to the shore came on.
He tried to challenge him to fight,
But Bāli found him to be light,
And clipped him underneath his belt,
As he from coast to coast did pelt.
Then to Kishkindha he returned,
And Ravan for his friendship yearned.
They were brothers by the fire;
An alliance did transpire.

35

But Hanuman in strength surpassed
All the beings of the past.
As a child just newly born
By hunger he was tossed and torn.
Seeking to obtain some fruit,
He chased the sun in close pursuit.
But Indra who perceived him there
Cast him down without a care.
To the earth that baby fell
Motionless, just like a shell.
Vayu was that baby's sire,
Outraged, he was filled with ire.
He took his son into a cave,
And he who to all creatures gave
Life, withdrew his moving force,
And every prana stayed its course.
All beings on the earth felt pain,
When Vayu had refused to reign.
To Brahmaloka devas went
They did of their state repent.
When they learned the reason why
Vayu left them all to die—
That his son had been assaulted

By Devendra who was faulted—
They petitioned to the wind
His living breath on them to send.

36

With Brahma at the deva's head,
They approached the child who's dead.
Brahmadeva did caress
The child who woke as He did press.
Vayu once again did blow
Relieving all the creature's woe.
Many were the boons they gave,
Trying to each other save.
The King of Devas then did place
His garland round that baby's face,
And said that thunderbolts could not
Harm him by its force or thought.
The sun bestowed on him his light,
Eloquence, and knowledge, right.
Varuna gave him many years,
And of his waters had no fears.
Invincible was Yama's gift,
In battle, death could not him lift,
And free he'd be from all disease,
Living fully and at ease.
Dhanada did give his mace,
At his service it would pace.
Vishwakarma gave the boon,
His weapons would not make him swoon.
Shiva and Lord Brahma spoke
Their weapons they could not evoke
On Hanuman, the Wind God's son,
Victorious would be that one.
He could change his form at will
And slay his foes through martial skill.
Hanuman, in mischief played

Havoc while the rishis prayed.
He scattered every implement,
With which their rites did supplement.
Disturbing altars and the fire,
That banar did incite their ire.
The rishis laid on him a curse
For his actions quite subverse,
That ignorance would veil his mind,
His memory he could not find.
Until his nature be revealed,
When he needs his strength to wield.
Then docilely that banar ranged
And no one was by him estranged.
Sugriva was his closest friend,
From the first unto the end.
In knowledge Hanuman is great,
With Brihaspati does he rate.
The banars did the gods create,
To their mission expiate.
So the rishis, Raghav's guests,
Of that king then made requests
To take their leave and home return,
Their meeting now had to adjourn.
They would aid his sacrifice
And he would take their wise advice.

37

Homage was to Raghav paid,
Every honor on him laid.
Happily his time was spent
And his kingdom did augment.

38

Many were the kings that came,
When Raghav did his throne reclaim.
Having honored all his guests

And fulfilled all their behests,
He bid to them a fond farewell,
Homeward they returned to dwell.

39

When Bharat learned of Raghav's plight,
He gathered all the kings to fight,
But Ramachandra had then slain
That demon, winning his campaign.
So happily they did return
Homeward bound their hearts did yearn.
Bhalukas and banars there,
Whom the love of Ram did share,
Were honored with great wealth and gems,
And finally took leave of him.

40

Bibhishan did Ram embrace,
His head upon Ram's feet did place,
And everyone assembled there,
Bowed to Ram upon his chair.
And many were the tears and cries,
Escaping from their muffled sighs.
And Ram did every one embrace,
As they moved to leave that place.
As long as Ram is ever heard,
By song or pen or spoken word,
Hanuman shall range the earth,
Where Ram is loved, there he shall berth.

41

Pushpak did to Ram return,
For Dhanada again did turn
The car to serve King Raghav's whim
For Dhanada did cherish him.
Ram adored that gracious car,

And sent it where it willed, afar.
As Ram upon the earth did reign,
Felicity did all obtain.
The people lived without disease,
And mothers birthed with grace and ease,
And the earth her grains did yield
Abundantly in every field.
The people all did love their king
For happiness to them did bring.

42

Ram and Sita passed their days
In many very pleasant ways.
Blessings did the Lord bestow,
For Sita, full with child did grow.
Ram was happy and fulfilled,
Prosperity to him did yield.
Celestial damsels danced for them,
And Ram obeyed her every whim.
Her beauty every day did grow;
Eternally their love did flow.
And Ram fulfilled her least desire,
Pleased to be her children's sire.
Sita longed to touch the feet
Of the sages they did meet
In their sacred hermitage,
Amid the thickened foliage.
On the morrow she would go
To greet the sages they did know.

43

Among his friends Ram paused to ask
A question that did pose a task:
What do people say about
Their king, who did the demons rout?
In truth his counselors replied,

That he was praised from every side
For his feats that came to pass;
His ancestors he did surpass.
In strength and courage he was best
And as his subjects, they were blessed.
But some among them cast a doubt
On Sita, who was so devout.
Since Ravan did his consort take,
Her purity was now at stake.
When their wives became impure
This they would have to endure
Because their king had done the same,
For this his subjects did him blame.
Ram was stricken down with grief,
Like a ship upon a reef,
When he heard their fateful word,
That was truly undeserved.

44

Raghav's eyes with tears were rimmed,
His luster and his brilliance dimmed.
He called his brothers to his side,
They who did with him reside.
When they looked upon his face,
Sorrow did his smile replace.
And silently the three did wait
To hear what Ram would then relate.
He held each one in close embrace,
And said his trust in them did place.
Yet burning tears did fill his eyes,
Amid his sobs and scorching sighs.

45

"You are aware how I did fight
The King of Titans, and him smite.
When Sita was alone he stole

My wife who is my ancient soul.
He bore her far away from us,
We pursued and found her thus.
Her innocence is pure and clean,
There is no fault in her to glean.
Her purity she did attest,
By entering the fiery test,
And all the gods proclaimed her true,
In purity and conduct too.
Yet the people do me blame,
For this they have disdained my name.
The price of honor is too high,
Yet for honor I would die.
My mind is set and will resolved,
To the way things have evolved.
He who would attempt to change
My mind himself he will estrange.
Lakshman do I now command
To lead Vaidehi from the land,
And of this act you should not speak,
This is the trust in you I seek.
Valmiki's ashram is not far
It is a sacred reservoir.
Vaidehi did request of me
To once again the sages see.
Now her wish you can fulfill,
In this you shall do as I will."
Saying so Kakutstha cried,
But they would not their thoughts confide.

46

The dawn did break upon the day,
And pity did Prince Lakshman sway.
Sumantra did ascend the car
Though sorrow did that Raghu mar.
Janaki did take her seat,

Eager to the sages greet,
But inauspicious signs drew near,
And for King Raghav did she fear.
The Ganga soon they sailed across
And sorrow did Prince Lakshman toss.

47

They upon the shore did land,
And Lakshman bowed with folded hand.
Bitterly Prince Lakshman wept,
He who was by sorrow swept.
He fell before her lotus feet,
And her forgiveness did entreat.
By King Raghav's cruel command
This excursion had been planned.
Ram was censured by his own
People, who did not condone
Reclaiming her to be his wife;
Among them it created rife.
They believed her to be pure;
The citizens could not be sure,
And now she would be sent away,
With Valmiki would she stay.
Valmiki would become her shelter;
He would be her benefactor.

48

To the earth she senseless fell,
As if the toll of death did knell.
When she from her swoon awoke,
These the words to him she spoke:
"What crime did I in past commit,
That misfortunes with me sit?
Did I separate a wife
From her husband in some life?
In the forest we did dwell,

Happily it fared us well.
But how can I now live alone
My future life to me unknown?
Dishonor has he always feared,
And now the same my flesh has seared.
Once my refuge, now he's cast
Me adrift without a mast.
Lakshman, please, you must this do,
For my sake do see it through.
Pay obeisance to my mothers,
And to all thy valiant brothers.
To Sri Ram, please touch his feet,
My words you must to him repeat:
'A woman's husband is her lord,
He is the ship a wife does board.
The tides of fate upon them sweep,
Sometimes high and sometimes deep.
The love that fills your manly breast
Should be shared with all the rest.
Your subjects are your brothers too,
This your dharma to pursue.'
Oh Prince Lakshman, do attest
My womb with child is fully blessed.
Do King Raghav's will obey,
So now return without delay."
Lakshman slowly bowed his head,
Reflecting on the words she said,
But he had never raised his eyes
Above her ankles in this wise.
Her pregnancy he did not know;
Bitter-sweet became his woe.
Lakshman had the river crossed,
His heart the while was tempest-tossed.
And Vaidehi lamely walked,
Misfortune had that devi stalked.

49

Valmiki then became aware
That Lakshman left Vaidehi there,
And he did go to seek that one
Where sorrow through her life did run.
Through tapas he could ascertain
Misfortune did on Sita rain.
He took her to the women's home,
Where female munis chanted _Om_,
And they would serve and worship her
And blessings on her did confer.

50

As Prince Lakshman went away
Destiny he did relay.
Fate had cast its awesome die,
And Prince Lakshman wondered why.
Sumantra to that hero spoke
The fate Durvasa did evoke.

51

Long ago his sire did go
To seek Vashishtha's face aglow.
Durvasa waited by his side,
There did righteousness abide.
Dasharatha asked him then
The future of his kith and kin.
Whereby that rishi did reply
With words that do today apply.
When suras and asuras fought,
The help of Vishnu, devas sought.
Asuras did with Bhrigu dwell
And Bhrigu's wife did keep them well.
Vishnu did remove her head
With his disc so she was dead.
Bhrigu muni cursed him there

That he would feel his heart's despair.
Born among the men he'd be
A prey to fate and destiny,
Separated from his wife,
He would live a lonely life.
Durvasa did this tale relate
Of why Ram would be cursed by fate.
But Ram would have two sons in life
By his chaste and pious wife.

52

Lakshman fell at Raghav's feet,
But Ram could not a word entreat.
Tears did fill his lotus eyes
That burned his cheeks and scorched his sighs.
Lakshman did beseech that one,
Whose luster dimmed the cloudy sun:
Surrender not unto his grief,
For Lakshman had a firm belief
To be detached in all of life,
Especially one's wealth or wife.
Then the two embraced each other;
Deeply they loved one another.

53

Raghav reassumed his duty,
He who was endowed with beauty,
And a story he retold
That through the ages had grown old.
Nriga was a famous king,
Prosperity to all did bring.
A thousand cows he gave away
In charity as was his way.
By accident a cow had strayed
Into a herd that was arrayed.
Coming from a distant land

'Twas given to another's hand.
When the brahmin found his cow,
An argument he did allow.
They approached their righteous king,
A settlement they hoped he'd bring.
But when he did refuse to meet,
The brahmin's wrath was then complete,
Cursing Nriga to become
A lizard 'til the Lord did come.
Invisible, within a well
Is where that monarch now would dwell.
So Ram did seek to arbitrate
Where duty did necessitate.

54

Lakshman did inquire to know
The end of Nriga's trials and woe.
So Raghav to him gave reply,
That Nriga, in his well did lie.
And placed his son upon the throne,
His deference to him was shown.

55

Ram another story told,
Equally revered and old.
Nimi was Ikshvaku's son,
His father's kingdom did he run.
A sacrifice he did begin,
Beneficial unto men.
The sage Vashishtha he did ask,
To preside above this task.
The muni said when he was free,
The sacrifice he would then see.
But Nimi would not wait to ask
Another sage to take the task.
Years had passed and then he came,

Vashishtha, to perform the same.
When he learned one did preside
He was subject to his pride
And cursed King Nimi to be dead,
And Nimi cursed him in his stead.
Then both the king and rishi fell
Lifeless, like a broken bell.

56

Vashishtha with his body shorn,
Approached the God who did adorn
With mala, veda, and the swan,
He wished a body now to don.
Swayambhu told him to go
And in the vital force to flow
Of Varuna as his seed,
If a body he did need.
Urvashi, a celestial maid,
Mischievously she did wade
In the waters of that king
And keen desire on him did bring.
She would not with him unite,
Since Mitra did her so invite.
So Varuna loosed his fire,
To satisfy intense desire
In a vessel Brahma made,
So his seed in there was laid.
Mitra by this was incensed,
His anger on her was dispensed.
He sent Urvashi to the world
Of men with curses that he hurled.
With Pururavas she was wed,
A son did issue from their bed.
Ayu then did have a son,
The family name through him did run.

Urvashi to her home returned,
Freedom from the earth was earned.

57

Mitra also loosed his seed
Into that vessel he did heed.
From that jar two sages came,
Ascending like a smokeless flame.
Agastya and Vashishtha, born,
Had their human bodies worn.
Nimi's body was preserved
By the rishis whom he served.
His consciousness does now reside
In the blinking of the eye.
To perpetuate his race,
His body, on the altar place
Was churned by those illustrious souls,
Who the rite of fire extols.
The ancient Janaka did stand,
The ancestor of Sita's land.

58

King Yayāti had two wives
And they were jealous of their lives.
The one who was disdained by him
Was subject to great ire and whim.
Threatening to end her life
Because he loved his other wife,
Her father laid on him a curse,
Cruel and strange, it was perverse.
Though young in years, he now was old,
Because the curse the rishi told.

59

Yayāti did approach each son,
He whom age did fall upon,

To ask them if they would betake
His age, and of their youth forsake.
Yadu did refuse the task,
But Puru did his father ask,
And gave his youth unto his sire
So he could satisfy desire.
Decrepitude his son did seek
To honor what his sire did speak.
After many years had lapsed
On his father it relapsed.
With Puru he was gratified
Because his wish was satisfied.
But Yadu did receive his curse,
That all his line would be perverse;
Cruel and mean, all would them scorn,
Though of his seed they had been born.
Puru was installed as king;
Felicity from him did spring.

60

Many sages came to see
Raghav of sagacity,
And Ram received them as his guests,
Obedient to their behests.

61

Long ago a demon named
Madhu was for valor famed.
Of the gods he was their friend,
And served the sages for their end.
From Rudra he received a gift
A trident both precise and swift.
This weapon would slay all his foes,
This trident from the Lord's arose.
If used against the twice-born men,
The trident would to Shiva spin.

To his son this spear had passed,
Until it would return at last.
Lavan is that demon's son,
Perverse and cruelly is he spun.
Now he does the sages taunt,
Rudra's weapon does he flaunt.
Of Ram the sages did request
Protection and that one arrest.

62

Shatrughan did Raghav ask,
Permission to accept this task.
And Raghav did agree within,
His wish to banish Lavan's men.
To install him as the king
Of Madhu, implements did bring.
When Shatrughan the demon slays,
The kingdom then upon him lays.

63

Shatrughan became the king;
Felicity to all did bring.
Raghunanda told him how
He could slay that demon now.
A shaft of Brahma he did give
That would not its foe forgive.
This weapon should be used again,
Then the battle he would win.
But only if he fought that one
When the brilliant morning sun
Had come and he did search for food,
And Shiva's weapon did occlude.
The weapon would be left inside,
While Lavan ranged the countryside.
Otherwise he cannot smite
That demon, once engaged to fight.

64

Ram bestowed an infantry,
Great elephants, and cavalry,
Upon his brother as he went
Upon the mission he was sent.
He should approach in such a way
That unaware his foe does stray
From the fort and leave behind
The weapon that no one can bind.
With the words Ram did impart,
Shatrughan with grace did part.

65

For many weeks they travelled far,
And camped beside a reservoir.
Then Shatrughan alone did roam
To greet Valmiki at his home.
Valmiki did receive his guest,
Attentive to his least request.
Of Saudasa he told a tale
Of the curse he did travail.
Saudasa, a valiant king,
Who justice to his own did bring,
Was passing through a thickened wood
When hungry tigers nearby stood.
They had eaten all the deer,
And purged the land both far and near.
The tigers traveled in disguise,
For they were demons in this guise.
In his anger he did kill
One tiger with his archer's skill.
The other demon swore revenge,
This treachery he would avenge.
Disappearing on the spot,
Saudasa of this forgot.
A sacrifice that king began,

Across the land as he did plan,
And many years did pass like this,
Until it all did go amiss.
That rakshasa, his former foe,
Dissension did among them sow.
Vashishtha's form he did assume,
To ask for meat he did presume.
As the cook, that demon came
With human flesh to cook the same.
The monarch's cooks prepared the meat
Unaware of the deceit.
Saudasa prepared the dish,
According to his guru's wish,
But Vashishtha burned with ire,
His anger smoldered like a fire.
He laid a curse upon the king,
Because he human flesh did bring,
That such would now become his food,
Saudasa in anger brewed.
He raised the water in his hand,
A curse upon his guru planned.
His consort then convinced the king
Misfortune would this action bring.
They did propitiate their priest,
The demon had prepared the feast,
So Vashishtha gave a boon,
The curse would vanish very soon.
Twelve years would he roam about,
Then from the curse he would come out,
And he would not remember what
Had passed, in his most fateful lot.

66

Shatrughan did pass the night,
And pleasant tidings came to light,
With twins Vaidehi had been blest,

Joy did them all invest.
Valmiki did perform the rites
Of those two effulgent lights,
With kusha grass they both were cleaned,
From this act their names were gleaned.
Kush and Lav they both were named,
And in the worlds they would be famed.
Shatrughan did blessings give,
That long of life they both would live.
Then he continued on his way,
For still he had to Lavan slay.

67

Shatrughan had passed a hut
And Chayvan did that prince instruct.
His ancestor had sought to fight
This wicked rakshasa of might,
But by his weapon was succumbed,
And to the bode of death had plumbed.
Before the demon takes his spear
Shatrughan must that one sear.
The rod of Shiva all does burn,
There is none who can it spurn.

68

Shatrughan did quickly go
Intent to slay this demon foe.
At the gate he did there wait
As Lavan did his hunger sate.
When he returned before his fort,
Shatrughan with him did sport.
He challenged him a single duel,
And Lavan thought he was a fool.
For his weapon he did go,
But Shatrughan had stopped his foe.

There he waited at the gate
Destiny did him await.

69

Lavan was incensed with rage,
And so their battle did engage.
The trees he threw upon his foe,
Were severed by his shaft and blow.
Then Lavan struck that hero's head,
And he fell down as if he's dead.
But once again he rose to fight,
Determined to that demon smite.
The weapon Brahma made he chose,
And trepidation then arose
Amongst the heavens and the sea,
The weapon blazed voraciously.
Shatrughan had loosed that dart
Which passed directly through his heart,
And like a tower Lavan fell,
Visiting the depths of hell.
Rudra's trident then returned,
To Shiva it again was turned.

70

The devas all did hail the prince,
Who that demon did dispense.
Then Shatrughan the kingdom reigned,
Prosperity had that one gained.
Twelve years there he quickly passed,
His happiness was unsurpassed.
But now he did so long to see
Raghav in his majesty.

71

With an escort he did go
To seek that Slayer of His Foe,

And at Valmiki's ashram stayed
Where the munis always prayed.
Valmiki bore a great affection
For this prince of Raghu's section,
And his prowess he had praised,
For Lavan had by him been razed.
And when they visited that sage,
In wondrous chants they did engage
Retelling all of Raghav's life,
His victories and all his strife.
It was as if before their eyes,
A dream of Raghav swiftly flies.
Marvelous 'twas to behold,
The life of Ram again retold.

72

To Ayodhya they did go,
To Him who does remove all woe,
And Shatrughan to Ram did bow,
Accomplishing what he did vow.
Shatrughan then asked his brother
Could they stay with one another?
Raghav gave a wise reply,
His people do on him rely.
The duty of a king is such
That he must love them overmuch
And sacrifice his love to serve
His people, and to never swerve.
So it was that Raghav planned
That Shatrughan across land,
Should serve his kingdom and remain
At Madhupur, where he would reign.
Shatrughan a week did stay,
Then for Madhupur made way.

73

For many years King Raghav reigned,
Felicity they all had gained.
Then a brahmin wept outside
Because his youthful son had died.
Somewhere did the king commit
A sin that he did not admit.
That is why their son had died,
So the brahmin to all cried.
He, his wife would die of grief,
Firm they were in this belief.

74

Raghav called the sages there
For he was caught in grave despair,
To hear from them the reason why
This brahmin's youthful son did die.
In _Krita yug_ is tapas cast
Only in the brahmin caste.
In _Treta yug_ it then had passed
To kshatriya and brahmin caste.
In _Dwapara_, great feats can be
Practiced in the castes of three.
In _Kali yug_ all four can be
Engaged in tapas easily.
But in Raghav's kingdom one
Shudra did infringe upon
A form of tapas and did cast
A stain upon King Raghav's past.
Ram should now his kingdom see,
And cast aside perversity.

75

Raghav called that mighty car,
Pushpak, which had traveled far,
And it returned at his command

Appearing at King Raghav's hand.
On that car he went to see
His kingdom in entirety,
Searching for an act amiss,
Leading to ungodliness.
An ascetic he espied,
Upside down he did abide,
And Raghav did that one contend,
Why he did his time so spend?
To what caste did he belong,
And had he practiced there for long?
What boon did he wish to gain;
Could his wishes he obtain?

76

That ascetic did desire
A boon received from heaven's sire
To ascend to Indra's door,
In the body that he wore.
From a shudra he was born,
But Raghav did not him forewarn.
With his sword he cut his head,
And that ascetic lay there dead.
Flowers from the heavens poured
On Raghav, whom they all adored.
Now that shudra was no threat,
The devas were with glee beset,
And that brahmin's child was healed,
The origin had been revealed.
With the devas Raghav went
Where Agastya had so spent
Twelve years underneath a lake,
And now he would from there awake.
Like the rising sun he rose,
In splendor he like amber glows.
They paid obeisance to that sage

Whose senses he did there assuage.
A bracelet on his arm did glow,
And on King Raghav did bestow
That celestial ornament,
At that most divine event.

77

Once Agastya muni stayed
Within a wood where none had strayed.
Lacking man and even beast,
In solitude it was a feast.
The air was laden with the scent
And fragrances that blossoms sent.
Rich in fruits and roots it stood,
That uninhabited, vast wood.
The waters of the lake were still,
Tranquility it did instill.
A fattened corpse on there did float,
Whose waters did its belly bloat,
And from the sky a car appeared,
More beautiful as it had neared.
A handsome youth therein did stand,
With apsaras at his hand.
From that car did he descend,
And of that corpse did make an end,
As his hunger he did sate,
With the flesh of him he ate.
The muni could not see the plan,
What possessed this handsome man
To take of this forbidden food,
The question in his mind did brood.

78

That being did address the sage,
His hunger he could not assuage.
That body was his mortal flesh,

Its bonds the being did enmesh.
Daily on this food he fed,
His body that to all was dead.
A rigid penance had he passed
Attaining brahmaloka last.
A gift to others he had not
Given or dispersed in thought.
Unsated by this food and thirst;
In laws of karma he was versed.
Agastya could that being save,
If he would take what he so gave.
And then a bracelet did he place,
That Vishwakarma once did trace,
In Agastya muni's hand
As Brahmadeva had so planned.
His mortal flesh did disappear,
Emancipated from that bier.

79

Ikshvaku ruled his father's kingdom,
Manu then left for his sanctum.
Hundred sons Ikshvaku sired,
Fulfilling what he had desired.
His youngest son was Daṇḍa named,
He was as a dullard famed.
Shukradeva was his guide,
His guru who did there reside.

80

As Daṇḍa roamed around the wood
A young and lovely damsel stood,
Unrivalled in her graceful form,
The shafts of Kāma did him swarm.
Aruja was the beauty's name,
His guru and her sire the same.
Daṇḍa was besieged with lust,

And on that virgin he was thrust.
He left her trembling standing there
And to his kingdom did repair.

81

Shukracharya was confused
When hearing that she was abused,
And laid a curse upon that king
That Indra would a dust storm bring.
His kingdom, home and all he cherished,
Would in seven days be perished.
And they left that sylvan range
Before the luscious land would change.
Now a desert there did stand,
And they moved on across the land.

82

And thus Agastya muni spoke
And inspiration did evoke.
Then Raghav to his home returned,
Where the people for him yearned.
Pushpak he dismissed with care
As it ascended in the air.

83

Bharat, Lakshman, Ram did call
To take advice from them withal.
Ram decided to begin
A sacrifice known unto men
As rajasuya of great fame,
Though it was difficult to claim.
Bharat to Sri Ram did say
The earth with him already lay.
He was the refuge of each king,
Protection he did to them bring.
How could he this campaign start,

When destruction it would chart?
Many houses would then fall
With the heroes he would call.
So Raghav listened to his friend,
The rajasuya did rescind,
For Bharat's counsel was quite true,
And he would not this rite pursue.

84

The ashwamedha rite erases
Sins, impurity effaces.
Lakshman gave him good advice
This rite would all his ends suffice.
Indra is for slaying famed,
A brahmin who was Vritra named.
A daitya, he was kind and good,
Three hundred leagues above he stood.
A rigid penance he pursued,
Where his senses were subdued.
Indra was quite insecure,
That Vritra would his throne secure.
To Vishnu, Indra gave appeal:
His kingdom they should not repeal.

85

Vishnu would not fight again,
For He protects the brahmin men,
His essence would with Indra ride,
Death would soon that one betide.
Brilliant like the rising sun,
Indra killed that pious one
As he sat in meditation,
Indra had no hesitation.
Sin that deva did pursue,
And Indra of his act did rue.

The ashwamedha sacrifice,
Could liberate Devendra's vice.

86

Brahminicide with Indra slept,
The earth and devas thereby wept.
The rain no longer flowed to earth,
And grains and forests had no worth.
The devas undertook the rite,
The sin from Indra did alight.
One fourth of the sin does dwell
With flooding rivers as they swell.
Another fourth fell to the earth
As salty dirt; it has no worth.
With women still a portion lives,
When their menstruation gives.
Those who do of brahmins lie
The final fourth with them does vie.
So Indra did ascend his throne,
The sacrifice he did condone.
And peace again on earth did reign,
As Devendra brought the rain.

87

Ila's story Ram next told,
As marvelous as it was old.
Ila was this monarch's name,
He was hunting for some game
And Hara in the wood did sport
With Uma, his divine consort.
All who entered in that wood,
Instantly, a woman, stood.
Ila was with fright dismayed,
To see his gender re-arrayed.
To Mahadeva did he pray,
But Hara laughed as if in play.

Of Parvati, he did ask
This female form to please unmask.
To his wish she did concede,
For with his essence he did plead.
One month as a man would pass,
The next month he would be a lass.
As he lived his life this way,
His memory between would sway.

88-89

Ila was a haunting beauty
Casting off her manly duty.
Freely through the woods she ranged,
Not knowing she had been estranged.
Budha, in the river stays,
Practicing ascetic ways.
Once she came to take a bath;
Unveiled, her body crossed his path.
The pangs of love did burn his chest
When his eyes on her did rest.
When she left the rishi rose,
And wandered back to his repose.
He called her to his hermitage
And asked to know her parentage.
She only knew she roamed at will,
Memory in her was still.
The truth to Budha came to light,
Foreknowing it through subtle sight.
In dalliance the two did spend
Their time, until the month did end.
Then as a man she did return,
To see his kingdom he did yearn.
But Budha did convince his guest
That after one year he'd be blessed,
If his time he would here spend
Until his tapas he did end.

So one month did pass away
Again the beauty came to stay.
In dalliance they spent their time,
And so the clock of fate did chime.
Nine months passed and gave a son,
Pururavas was that one.

90

Many rishis gathered there,
A sacrifice they did prepare.
The ashwamedha they performed,
And Ila was again transformed.
Once again his manhood came,
His kingdom did no longer claim,
Then to Pratisthana went,
And Pururavas with him sent.

91

So King Raghav did prepare
To perform that service there.
The brilliant rishis all assembled,
Hundred suns they all resembled.
Kings and rishis also joined
In the sacrifice conjoined.
Sugriva and the banars came,
And Bibhishan did do the same.
Many structures they had built
That with jewels and gold were gilt.
Gold and silver, food and wine,
All were given and some kine.
Ram made a statue of his wife,
As beautiful as she in life.
Everyone was satisfied;
Thereby Ram was gratified.

92

Ram did loose a mighty steed,
And Lakshman did that stallion heed.
For one year it freely ran
Unhindered as the priests did plan.
Anyone who wished for gems,
Or had some secret cherished whims,
Was fulfilled in every way,
And Raghav did in dharma stay.

93

Valmiki saw the sacrifice,
Resplendent like a paradise,
And Lav and Kush he asked to go,
The Ramayana there to sow.
With special fruits to soothe their voice,
Instruments that would revoice,
As they sang the haunting tale
The life of Ram they would unveil.
"Before the priests and sages sing,
Before the princes and the king,
With lilting tune and cheerful heart,
This epic should you both impart."
Valmiki counseled them again
To sing before the Best of Men.

94

In Ram's pavilion they did sing,
And tears unto their eyes did bring.
All who heard the lilting song
Did gaze upon the twins for long.
And many people loved the art
And how they could not tell apart
These young munis from the king,
As they lovingly did sing.
Gold and silver had they offered
To the twins this wealth was proffered.

But they did refuse the gold,
As Valmiki had them told.
What use in the woods is there
For gold, when roots make up their fare?
They asked to know who wrote this song,
To meet the author they did long.
Lav and Kush to this replied,
Valmiki, who did there abide,
Wrote this sacred, epic tale
Of Ramachandra's life to hail.

95

Ram for many days did hear
That song which moved them all to tear,
And after searching deep within,
He knew of them their origin.
Kush and Lav he recognized,
Born of him he had surmised.
If Sita was of conduct pure,
If free from sin she was secure,
He asked Valmiki then to bring
Vaidehi there before the king,
And by an oath she should proclaim
Her purity, to clear her name.
On the morrow they would wait
For Sita to approach the gate.

96

A multitude before him stood,
Motionless, they were like wood.
Rishis of exalted name,
And heroes of impressive fame,
And citizens from every caste
Gathered as the fates were cast.
Valmiki did approach the king,
And Janaki with him did bring.

The multitude broke out and cried
To see Vaidehi sorely tried.
Valmiki to the king did speak,
With Sita veiled in her mystique:
"I am Valmiki, known to thee,
Who brings before thee, Maithili.
Pure and chaste, I to thee swear
That Sita is beyond compare.
Her purity is known to thee,
And yet you feared some calumny,
And did abandon her, your wife,
So faithful to you all through life.
A lie has never crossed my speech,
And may my penance fruitless breach,
If what I speak here unto you,
That she is faithful, be not true.
In meditation I discerned
That out of fear you Sita spurned.
There is no fault in Janaki;
This I now say truthfully.
Lav and Kush, each one your son,
The Raghu blood in them does run."

97

Sita did before him stand
With lowered head and joined hand.
Then Ram unto the people spoke
The thoughts which Sita did evoke:
"With Valmiki, I agree,
In conduct and in purity
Sita is without compare,
Her piety is ever fair.
Her innocence did pass the test,
The God of Fire did this attest.
Because of public condemnation,
Sita suffered great privation.

Kush and Lav are both my heir,
And in my heart are welcome there.
Sita now to reconcile,
She who is bereft of guile,
Is why I called you here today,
To hear the oath that she would say."
A fragrant breeze did on them blow,
As if it could assuage her woe.
Sita softly did complete
Words both bitter and so sweet:
"If my speech you do believe,
Then may the earth my soul receive,
That Ram alone dwells in my heart,
From duty I did never part."
Then from the earth a throne arose
With gold and gems, amidst their throes,
And on the heads of nāgas laid
A seat with gold and silk brocade.
The Goddess Earth did wait to hold
Vaidehi, and her child enfold.
And with Vaidehi in her arms,
As if she did receive her alms,
They both descended into earth,
Where Brahma had ordained her birth.
The devas danced in great delight
To witness that auspicious sight,
And flowers from the heavens rained
As the people there remained.

98

Ram did stagger from the blow,
Flooded by a grievous woe.
He cursed the earth to give her back,
Or the earth he would attack.
She who suffered in the past
Was with her mother now at last.

Vaidehi, whom he once did spurn,
To see her now his soul did yearn.
But silently the earth replied,
And Sita dwelt with her inside.
Ram swore a vengeance to uphold,
If she did not release her hold.
Then Brahmadeva did appear,
And told King Raghav not to fear.
Within the earth she now would stay,
And she to Raghav now would pray.
His origin he should recall,
He was the source and hope of all.
Reunited they would be
Joined in great felicity.
Of this epic all should hear
Removing every doubt and fear.
The end of Raghav's life is told,
By he who subtle visions hold.
Valmiki wrote this epic tale
That all the gods and rishis hail.
Then with his children Raghav went,
And of Vaidehi did lament.

99

When the new day did arrive,
The kings and rishis did derive
Delight when hearing of the tale
That did of Raghav's life foretell.
Ten thousand years Sri Ram would reign,
And many rites he did ordain.
In charity he did engage,
With gifts to priests and every sage,
His people knew prosperity,
Enjoying felicity.
Raghav never married twice;
His love for Sita did suffice,

And used a statue of her form,
When sacrifices would perform.
In time his mothers passed away,
In devaloka they did stay,
Reunited with his sire
Fulfilling all of their desire.

100

Kaikeyi's brother sent Ram word
That of a country he had heard
Rich in fruits and fertile land,
The conquest of it should be planned.
Gandharvas did defend that space
Where their palaces held place,
And only Ram could them defeat,
So his uncle did entreat.
Bharat was by Ram appointed
And his two sons were anointed.
Ruling kingdoms in the land
When it was within their hand.
Bharat led an army vast,
As they journeyed out at last.

101

Yudhajit did join the force,
To flow along this fateful course.
The gandharvas they'd invade,
And death amongst them did pervade.
For seven days the battle raged,
And finally Bharat, enraged,
Did loose a mantra-driven shaft,
And many souls to death did draft.
Decisively he won the war,
And they did entertain no more
Gandharvas, but then seized the mast;
The citadels did fall at last.

Filled with parks and laden trees,
Delicious fruits, and gentle breeze,
The palaces were magical,
Embellishments, indelible.
Rich in wealth and precious gem,
These palaces were now with them.
The sons of Bharat were installed,
And he to Raghav was recalled.

102

Then Lakshman's sons he did install,
Kingdoms on them both did fall.
His two sons did thereby reign
In countries that Sri Ram did gain.
Happily the years did fly,
And time was swiftly passing by.

103

Death stood at King Raghav's gate,
An audience he did await.
Disguised as if a twice-born one,
His radiance exceeds the sun.
Lakshman did that one approach,
It was the king he wished to broach.
When Ramachandra was informed,
Unto his wishes he conformed.
An audience he did request
With him alone at his behest.
If one should overhear their speech,
The arm of death would that one reach.
Lakshman waited at the door,
So none could in that room cross o'er.

104

That messenger revealed his name,
For he was Death itself, the same.

The Grandsire of the World did send
His messenger to Raghav's end.
When Ram was born amongst the men,
Eleven thousand years therein,
Amongst the creatures of the earth,
For this he took a human birth.
When Ravan cast the worlds in fear,
Vishnu, on the earth was near.
Now Ram's mission was complete,
For Ram's return he did entreat.
The devas did request that God,
To shelter them beneath his rod.
And Raghav did approve the word,
That from Yama he had heard.

105

While Ram and Death together spoke,
Durvasa's wrath it did provoke.
Arriving at King Raghav's gate,
He had no patience there to wait,
And urgently did want to see
The Lord of Men most hastily.
Lakshman to that sage replied
That Ram was occupied inside.
He could not that king disturb,
But soon his wrath he could not curb.
He threatened to destroy his race,
If he did not his message place
And inform that righteous king,
That Durvasa did he bring.
Lakshman did reflect inside,
That good should all of them betide,
Better one should die than all,
And so King Raghav did he call.
The Lord of Death did take his leave,
And Raghav did the sage receive.

One thousand years the sage did fast
And now he wanted a repast.
So Ramachandra fed his guest,
Satisfying each behest.
To his ashram he returned,
And Raghav, full of grief was burned.

106

Lakshman then approached his brother,
They who dearly loved each other.
Honoring King Raghav's vow,
Lakshman to his death did bow.
Raghav was beset with grief,
Nowhere could he find relief.
His counsellors did Raghav call,
And told them what did him befall.
Vashishtha gave him sound advice,
To banish Lakshman would suffice.
For men who do revere their name,
Banishment or death's the same.
For dharma in the world to live,
This sentence did King Raghav give.
And Lakshman, full of sorrow, cried,
And left his brother's loving side.
To the Saryu river shore,
Lakshman went and came no more.
With his senses all controlled,
The devas had the prince extoled.
Then in the sky he disappeared,
The devas had the prince revered.

107

Drowning in a sea of sorrow,
Raghav did Prince Lakshman follow.
Calling Bharat to his side,
His purpose to him did confide.

Bharat did refuse the throne,
The kingdom never would he own.
Forever by his brother's side,
With Rahgav he would now reside.
To Shatrughan some soldiers went,
This action they did not repent.
The sons of Raghav did ascend
The throne to serve the people's end.
The citizens with grief did drop,
To think of death they did not stop.
With Raghav they did yearn to go,
Death with him they wished to know.
By the power of his grace,
They also death with him would face.

108

Shatrughan approached his brothers,
He would follow like the others.
Both his sons began to rule
The kingdom like a sacred jewel.
Bhalukas and banars there,
And titans did to Ram repair.
Gandharvas, rishis, and each god,
Resolved to follow where he trod.
Sugriva did install as king
Angada, to Raghav bring
Himself and banars to their lord,
For death with him they now would ford.
To Bibhishan King Raghav said
To govern Lanka in his stead.
While the sun above does shine,
His empire never would decline.
And Hanuman he told to stay
As long as people do Ram say,
And happily to range the world,
While his story is unfurled.

To Jamwant who received his care,
He would also settle there
Until the kali yug sets in,
He would live on earth with men.
Those who wished to follow then,
Proceeded with the Best of Men.

109

At the dawn King Raghav rose,
His life on earth he now would close.
The rishis, devas, followed him,
Women, children, all of them,
His brothers and his brother's wives,
Chose with him to end their lives.
The titans, banars, every beast
Did go with him, as did the least.
No one in the town remained,
Raghav had their lives sustained.
Silently King Raghav strode
Barefoot on that dusty road,
But all were full of happiness,
With Ram they felt delightful bliss.

110

The sandy shores of Saryu came,
And Brahma, like a brilliant flame,
Addressed Lord Vishnu there on earth
Who as a man had taken birth.
Ram's abode with Him did wait,
Eternally at heaven's gate.
All the brothers then did go
To heaven with their hearts aglow,
And all the devas called their name,
Proclaiming their eternal fame.
Every banar, beast and man,
Titan, to the river ran

Instantly they were absolved,
Saryu had their sins dissolved.
All of them to heaven went,
Even animals were sent.
Their pristine forms they did regain,
Those devas that on earth did reign.
Valmiki wrote this epic tale,
And Brahmadeva does it hail.
To purify and sanctify,
So it does one glorify.
Longevity, prosperity,
Attends on one with verity.
For he who does recite this tale
Adversity cannot prevail.
Glory to that ageless One
Resplendent like the peerless sun.

Om. Shantih, shantih, shantih.

GLOSSARY

ADITI. The mother of the gods and wife of Kashyap.

AGASTYA. A great rishi.

AGNIVARNA. A king in the line of Ikshvaku, son of Shankhan and father of Shighraga.

AHALYA. The wife of Gautam.

AJA. A king in the line of Ikshvaku, son of Yayāti and father of Dasharatha.

AKAMPAN. A rakshasa in Ravan's army.

AKSHA. A rakshasa, son of Ravan.

AMBARISHA. A king in the line of Ikshvaku, son of Prashurshruka and father of Nahusha.

ANARANYA. A king in the line of Ikshvaku, son of Bāṇa, father of Prithu.

ANASUYA. A great sage, the wife of Atri.

ANGADA. The son of Bāli and Tārā.

ANJANĀ. A nymph who was the mother of Hanuman.

ANSHUMAN. Son of Asamanjas and father of Dilip.

APSARAS. Celestial nymphs.

ARAṆYA KĀṆḌA. The section in the Ramayana that describes Ram's exile in the forest.

ARJUNA. A king who had a thousand arms, and who defeated Ravan.

ARUJA. The daughter of Shukradeva.

ASAMANJAS. Son of Sagara and Keshini, father of Anshuman. An evil king in the line of Ikshvaku.

ASHOKA GROVE. A garden in Ravan's capital where Sita was held captive.

ASHRAM. A hermitage.

ASITA. A king in the line of Ikshvaku, son of Bharata and father of Sagara.

ASURA. Daitya. Demon or titan.

ASHWAMEDHA SACRIFICE. A horse sacrifice.

ATIKAY. A rakshasa, son of Ravan.

ATRI. A great sage.

AYODHYA. The place of Ram's birth. The capital of Koshala.

AYODHYĀ KĀṆḌA. The section of the Ramayana that describes Ram's life in Ayodhya.

AYOMUKHI. A rakshasi.

AYU. The son of Pururavas and Urvashi.

AYURVEDA. Ancient herbal medicine.

BĀLA KĀṆḌA. The story of Ram's childhood.

BĀLI. An asura king who displaced Indra from the heavens. Son of Virochana, and devotee of Vishnu. Bāli is also the name of the banar king, Sugriva's older brother and son of Indra.

BĀṆA. A king in the line of Ikshvaku, son of Vikukshi, father of Anaranya.

BANAR. "Forest dweller," a race of intelligent beings whose hero, Hanuman, assisted Ram.

BEST OF MEN. One of the names of Ram (see RAM).

BHAGIRATHA. A king in the line of Ikshvaku, son of Dilip and father of Kakutstha.

BHAGIRATHI. The Ganges that followed Bhagiratha to earth.

BHALUKA. A race of men who were intelligent and whose faces resembled those of bears.

BHARADWAJA. A sage, disciple of Valmiki.

BHARAT (BHARTA). Ram's younger brother, son of Dasharatha and Kaikeyi, a partial incarnation of Vishnu.

BHARATA. A king in the line of Ikshvaku, son of Dhruvasamdhi and father of Asita.

BHAVA. One of the names of Shiva.

BHRIGU. A sage, son of Manu.

BIBHISHAN. A rakshasa, younger brother to Ravan. He became King of Lanka after Ravan's death.

BRAHMA or BRAHMADEVA. The creator of the universe.

BRAHMALOKA. The sphere where Brahma lives.

BRAHMARISHI. A divine sage.

BRAHMASIRA or BRAHMASTRA. A divine weapon created by Brahma, which uses the force of mantra.

BRAHMASTRA. A divine weapon created by Lord Brahma.

BRAHMIN. The priestly or scholarly caste.

BRAHMINICIDE. The sin of killing a brahmin.

BRIHADRATHA. A king in the line of Nimi, son of Devarata and father of Mahavir.

BRIHASPATI. The spiritual teacher of the gods.

BUDHA. A sage, (not the well-known Buddha).

CASTE. A social division among people in the Vedic times. There are four divisions: priest or brahmin, warrior or kshatriya, merchant or vaishya, and servant or shudra.

CHANDALA. One who tends the cremation ground.

CHAYVAN. A sage.

CHITRAKUTA. A mountain where Ram, Lakshman, and Sita lived while in exile.

CHULI. A sage, father of Brahmadatta.

DADHIMUKHA. A banar warrior who was protecting Madhuvan, the celestial grove of Sugriva.

DAITYA. Demons, titans.

DAKSHA. One of the mind-born sons of Brahma.

DĀNAVAS. A race of giants.

DANDA. One of the sons of Ikshvaku.

DANDAKA. A forest found between the rivers Godavari and Narmada where Ram, Lakshman, and Sita spent their exile.

DANU. A name for Kabandha.

DARSHAN. To have a glimpse of a saintly personage, or to be blessed by the presence of such a being.

DASHARATHA. The father of Ram, Bharat, Lakshman, and Shatrughan. The King of Ayodhya. Also known as Kakutstha, Raghu.

DASHANANA. One of the names of Ravan, son of Vishravas.

DĒVA. A bright being, demi-gods.

DEVALOKA. The realm of the gods.

DEVAMIDHA. A king in the line of Nimi, son of Kirtiratha and father of Vibudha.

DEVANTAKA. A rakshasa, son of Ravan.

DEVARATA. A king in the line of Nimi, son of Suketu and father of Brihadratha.

DEVENDRA. One of the names of Indra (see INDRA).

DEVI. A goddess.

DHANADA. One of the names of Vaishravana, brother of Ravan and son of Vishravas.

DHANVANTARI. The founder of Ayurveda.

DHARMA. Right action.

DHRISHTAKETU. A king in the line of Nimi, son of Sudhriti and father of Haryashva.

DHRUVASAMDHI. A king in the line of Ikshvaku, son of Susamdhi and father of Bharata.

DHUMRAKSHA. A rakshasa in Ravan's army.

DILIP. A king in the line of Ikshvaku, son of Anshuman and father of Bhagiratha.

DITI. Mother of the daityas, wife of Kashyap.

DUNDUBHI. A demon killed by the banar Bāli.

DURVASA. A sage.

DUSHANA. A demon, brother of Ravan.

DWAPARA YUG. The age where dharma is diminished by half.

GĀDHI. The son of Kushanabha and father of Vishwamitra.

GANDHARVA. Divine musicians.

GANGA. A sacred river, daughter of Himavat, sister of Uma, who descended to earth by passing through Shiva's hair. Also known as Ganges, Gangadevi.

GANGADEVI. One of the names of Ganga (see GANGA).

GARUDA. A divine bird.

GAUTAM. A divine sage, husband of Ahalya.

GAVAKSHA. A banar warrior.

GAVAYA. A banar warrior.

GELDING. The act of castrating a ram, horse or steer.

GOKARNA. An ashram

GRANDSIRE OF THE WORLD. One of the names of Brahma (see BRAHMA).

GUARDIAN OF WEALTH. A title for Vaishravana.

GUHA. King of the Nishadas, a tribe that lived on the border of Koshala.

GURU. A name for a spiritual teacher.

GURUDEVA. A bright being, a teacher.

GURUKULA. The ashram of the guru.

HANUMAN. The son of the Wind God and nymph Anjanā. A banar warrior, friend of Sugriva and devotee of Ram.

HARA. One of the names of Shiva (see SHIVA).

HARI. One of the names of Vishnu.

HARYASHVA. A king in the line of Nimi, son of Dhrishtaketu and father of Pratindhaka.

HEMA. A celestial nymph.

HIMACHAL. Himavat, King of the Himalayas, father of Ganga and Uma.

HIMAVAT. The King of Himalayas, father of Uma and Ganga.

HOUSE OF RAGHU. A name for Dasharatha's dynasty.

HRASVAROMA. A king in the line of Nimi, son of Svarnaroma and father of Janak.

IKSHVAKU. Founder of the Solar Race of Kings. The son of Manu.

ILA. A king whose gender was changed by Shiva, father of Pururavas.

ILVALA & VATAPI. Two demons that tried to kill Agastya.

INDRA. The King of the Gods. Also known as Devendra.

INDRAJIT. A rakshasa, son of Ravan, vanquisher of Indra, also known as Meghanad.

JĀBĀLI. A sage in the court of King Dasharatha who tried to convince Rama not to go into exile.

JAHNAVI. A river.

JAHNU. A sage who swallowed the Ganges.

JAMADAGNI. A sage, father of Parasuram.

JAMBAVAN. One of the banar generals.

JAMBUMALI. A rakshasa, son of Prahasta.

JAMWANT (JAMAWANT). The King of Bhalukas.

JANAKA. The King of Mithila, father of Sita, also known as Videha.

JANAKI. One of the names of Sita (see SITA).

JANASTHAN. A village of demons in the Daṇḍaka forest.

JAṬĀYU. King of Birds, friend of King Dasharatha, who was slain by Ravan while trying to protect Sita.

KABANDHA. A demon who was killed by Ram. He was a gandharva who was cursed by Indra for his pride. He told Ram where to find Sugriva.

KAIKASI. A rakshasi, daughter of Sumali who wed Vaishravas, mother of Ravan, Kumbhakarn, Shurpankha, and Bibhishan.

KAIKAYA. The tribe from which Queen Kaikeyi came.

KAIKEYA. The father of Queen Kaikeyi.

KAIKEYI. One of the Queens of Dasharatha and mother of Bharat.

KAILASHA MOUNTAIN. A sacred mountain. The highest mountain in the Himalayas.

KAKUTSTHA. A king in the line of Ikshvaku, son of Bhagiratha and father of Raghu. A name used for the descendants of Ikshvaku.

KALA MOUNTAIN. A mountain in the western region.

KALI YUG. The age where dharma is diminished by three-fourths.

KALINDI. A river.

KĀMA. Lust.

KANDA. A banar warrior.

KANDU. A sage.

KAPILA. A great sage, an incarnation of Vishnu.

KARTTIK. The son of Shiva. Also known as Skanda. The commander-in-chief of the god's army.

KASHYAP. A sage, grandson of Brahma and father of Vibhāndaka.

KAUSHALYA. One of King Dasharatha's queens and mother of Ram.

KAUSHIK. King Kaushik later became known as the sage Vishwamitra.

KAUSHIKI. Also known as Satyavati who became a river.

KAUSTUBHA. A divine gem worn by Lord Vishnu.

KESARĪ. The banar husband of Anjanā.

KESHINI. Queen of King Sagar, and mother of Asamanjas.

KHARA. A demon, brother of Ravan.

KINE. A term for cattle.

KING OF MITHILA. Janak, the father of Sita. Also known as Videha.

KING OF DEVAS. A name for Indra (see INDRA).

KING OF ANGA. Romapāda, the neighbor of King Dasharatha and father-in-law of the sage Rishyashringa.

KING OF GODS. Indra, the King of the Gods (see INDRA).

KING OF TITANS. A title of Ravan.

KING KUSHA. An ascetic king, the son of Brahma.

KING MARUTTA. A king whose sacrifice was obstructed by Ravan.

KIRTIRATHA. A king in the line of Nimi, son of Pratindhaka and father of Devamidha.

KIṢHKINDHĀ KĀṆḌA. The part of the Ramayana which describes Ram's meeting with Sugriva and Hanuman and the citadel Kishkindha.

KISHKINDHA. The land where the banar Bāli ruled and was later given to Sugriva by Ram.

KOSHALA. The country where Dasharatha reigned.

KRATHANA. A banar warrior.

KRAUNCHA BIRDS. A species of heron.

KRISHASHVA. He gave divine weapons to Vishwamitra.

KRITA YUG. The age where dharma is fully observed.

KRITTIKAS. The Pleiades, nurses of Karttik.

KSHATRIYA. The warrior caste.

KUKSHI. Son of Ikshvaku, father of Vikukshi.

KUMBHA. A rakshasa, son of Kumbhakarn.

KUMUDA. A banar warrior.

KUSHA GRASS. A sacred grass used in rituals.

KUSH. One of the twin sons of Ram and Sita.

KUSHA RIVER. A river where Diti performed austerities.

KUSHA. A son of Brahma and father of Kushanabha. Also one of the sons of Ram and Sita.

KUSHADVAJA. Younger brother to King Janak.

KUSHANABHA. A son of King Kusha.

KUVERA. The God of Wealth.

LAKE PAMPA. A lake where Ram and Lakshman rested while in exile.

LAKSHMAN (LAKSHMANA). The younger brother of Ram and Bharat, son of Dasharatha and Sumitra, a partial incarnation of Vishnu.

LAKSHMI. The divine consort of Vishnu. Sita was an incarnation of Lakshmi.

LAKSHMIDEVI. A name for Lakshmi, the consort of Vishnu.

LANKA. An island off the tip of South India which later became known as Ceylon and is now Sri Lanka. In the Ramayana, Lanka is the capital of Ravan, King of Titans.

LAV. One of the twin sons of Ram and Sita.

LAVAN. A rakshasa, son of Madhu, King of Madhupur.

LORD OF LAKSHMI. One of the names of Vishnu (see VISHNU).

LORD KRISHNA. An incarnation of Vishnu.

LOSHTA. A sage's begging bowl.

MADHU. A titan.

MADHUPUR. The kingdom of Lavan.

MADHUVAN. A celestial grove in Kishkindha.

MAHADEVA. One of the names of Shiva (see SHIVA).

MAHAPARSHWA. A rakshasa, brother of Ravan.

MAHARAKSHA. A rakshasa in Ravan's army.

MAHARISHI. A title for a great rishi.

MAHAROMA. A king in the line of Nimi, son of Mahidhraka and father of Svarnaroma.

MAHAVIR. A king in the line of Nimi, son of Brihadratha and father of Sudhriti.

MAHENDRA. A mountain.

MAHESHWARA. One of the names of Shiva.

MAHIDRAKA. A king in the line of Nimi, son of Vibudha and father of Maharoma.

MAHODARA. A rakshasa in Ravan's army, brother of Ravan.

MAHODAYA MOUNTAIN. A mountain where sacred healing herbs grew.

MAINĀKA. A mountain hidden in the ocean.

MAITHILI. One of the names of Sita (see SITA).

MALI. A rakshasa, son of Sukesha, brother of Malyavan and Sumali.

MALYAVAN. A rakshasa, the grandfather of Ravan on his mother's side. Also the son of Sukesha, and the brother of Sumali and Mali.

MANDAKINI. A river by Chitrakuta Mountain.

MANDARA MOUNTAIN. This mountain was used to churn the milky ocean.

MANDARKINI. A sage.

MĀNDAVĪ. The wife of Bharat, daughter of King Kushadvaja.

MANDHATA. A king in the line of Ikshvaku, son of Yuvanashva and father of Susamdhi.

MANDODARI. The favorite queen of Ravan.

MANTHARĀ. The maid of Queen Kaikeyi, who was a hunchback.

MANU. The first man, the law giver.

MARICHA. A rakshasa.

MARICHI. One of the mind-born sons of Brahma.

MARU. A king in the line of Ikshvaku, son of Shighraga and father of Prashurshruka.

MARUTS. Gods of the tempest, sons of Diti, helpers of Indra.

MATANGA. A sage.

MATTA. A rakshasa, brother of Ravan.

MĀYĀ. The veiling power of the Lord. A giant who made a supernatural cavern.

MĀYĀVĪ. A demon killed by the monkey Bāli.

MEGHANAD. One of the names of Indrajit, son of Ravan.

MENAKĀ. A celestial nymph who tempted the sage Vishwamitra.

MERU MOUNTAIN. A sacred mountain.

MILKY OCEAN. The ocean the suras and asuras churned for divine nectar.

MITHI. The son of King Nimi, father of Janaka.

MITHILA. The land ruled by King Janak.

MITRA. A deva.

MOHINI. An incarnation of Lord Vishnu as a woman used to delude the asuras and steal the nectar of immortality.

MUNI. A sage.

NĀGA. A being of the serpent race.

NAHUSHA. A king in the line of Ikshvaku, son of Ambarisha and father of Yayāti.

NALA. A banar who was the son of Vishvakarma.

NALAKUVARA. A sage, the son of Vaishravana.

NANDI. The mount of Shiva.

NANDIGRAMA. The village where Bharat lived while Ram was in exile.

NANDIVARDHAN. A king in the line of Nimi, son of Udavasu and father of Suketu.

NARAD. Mind-born son of Brahma who has power to travel in the three worlds. A divine sage.

NARAKA. Literally means hell, but there was also a giant named Naraka.

NARANTAKA. A rakshasa, son of Ravan.

NARAYAN. One of the names of Lord Vishnu (see VISHNU).

NIKUMBHA. A rakshasa, son of Kumbhakarn.

NIKUMBHILA GROVE. A grove in Lanka where Indrajit performed sacrifices.

NILA. A banar general who was the son of Agni.

NIMI. The first king in the line of Janak's dynasty, father of Mithi.

NISHAKARA. A sage who knew Jaṭāyu and Sampāti.

NRIGA. A king who was cursed and became a lizard.

NYAGRODHA TREE. A sacred fig tree.

OJAS. Semen.

OM. A sacred syllable of Vedic texts.

PANASA. A banar warrior.

PANCHAPSARA. A lake with five nymphs where the sage Mandarkini lived.

PANCHAVATI. An area close to the Godavari river.

PARAMRISHI. Title given to a great rishi.

PARASURAM. An incarnation of Vishnu, son of Jamadagni and Renuka.

PARVATI. The divine consort of Shiva, also known as Uma.

PAYASA. A sweet dish made from rice and milk.

PITRIS. Ancestors.

PULASTYA. Ravan's grandfather, one of the mind-born sons of Brahma.

PRAHASTA. A rakshasa, one of the ministers of Ravan.

PRAHETI & HETI. The first two rakshasas.

PRASHURSHRUKA. A king in the line of Ikshvaku, son of Maru and father of Ambarisha.

PRATINDHAKA. A king in the line of Nimi, son of Haryashva and father of Kirtiratha.

PRATISTHANA. The kingdom where Ila and Pururavas reigned.

PRAVRIDHA. A king in the line of Ikshvaku, son of Raghu and father of Sudarshan.

PRICKET. A young male deer.

PROWLERS OF THE NIGHT. A title for titans, rakshasas, demons.

PUROSHOTTAM. Narayan.

PURU. The son of Yayāti who bore his father's curse in his stead.

PURURAVAS. The son of Budha, whom Urvashi married.

PUSHKARA. A sacred place where Visvamitra practiced austerity.

PUSHPAK. A divine car that could travel the worlds at will.

RAGHAV. One of the names of Ram (see RAM). A title for those in the House of Raghu.

RAGHU. A king in the line of Ikshvaku, son of Kakutstha and father of Pravridha. A title for those in the House of Raghu.

RAJARISHI. A title for kingly sages.

RAJASUYA. A sacrifice performed by kings to attain sovereignty over the world.

RAKSHASA. A demon, titan.

RAKSHASI. A female demon.

RAM (RAMA). An avatar of Vishnu. Also known as Sri Ram, Raghav, Kakutstha, Raghu, Raghunanda, Ramachandra, Best of Men, Joy of the House of Raghu.

RAMACHANDRA. One of the names of Ram (see RAM). The "moon-faced one"

RAMAYANA. The story of Ram.

RAMBHA. A celestial nymph who tried to tempt the sage Vishwamitra. Also the name of a banar warrior.

RASĀTALA. A hell found at the bottom of the sea.

RAVAN (RAVANA). The King of Titans in Lanka. The rakshasa who abducted Sita.

RICHIKA. A sage.

RISHI. A yogi, saint, muni, seer.

RISHYAMUKA. The mountain where Sugriva was hiding.

RISHYASHRINGA. A sage who performed the sacred rite for Dasharatha to acquire sons. Son of Vibhāndaka.

ROD OF BRAHMA. A divine weapon created by the Lord Brahma.

ROMAPĀDA. A king in the line of Janaka.

RUDRA. One of the names of Shiva (see SHIVA).

SAGAR. A king in the line of Ikshvaku. Father of Asamanjas. Also a name of the Ocean.

SĀLAKATANKATĀ. The wife of Vidyutkesha.

SAMKASHYA. A neighboring land to Mithila.

SAMPĀTĪ. Brother of Jatāyu, a raptor whose wings had been burned by the sun.

SAMROCANA. A banar warrior.

SANNĀDANA. A mighty warrior of the race of bhalukas.

SAPTAJANAS. A holy ashram where seven sages lived.

SĀRANA. A rakshasa who was sent by Ravan to spy on the banar force.

SARASWATI. The goddess of learning.

SARYU. A sacred river.

SATYAVATI. Daughter of King Gādhi, sister of Vishwamitra.

SAUDASA. A king who was cursed by Vashishtha for feeding him human flesh.

SAVITRA. A warrior in the deva's army who killed Sumali.

SHABALA. Sage Vashishtha's sacred cow, the wish-fulfilling cow; also called Kamadhenu.

SHANKAN. A king in the line of Ikshvaku, son of Sudarshan and father of Agnivarna.

SHARABHA. A banar warrior.

SHARABHANGA. A saint.

SHARDULA. A rakshasa, spy of Ravan.

SHASTRA. Sacred scriptures.

SHATANAND. A sage. The son of Gautam and Ahalya.

SHATRUGHAN. The youngest brother of Ram, twin brother of Lakshman, son of Dasharatha and Sumitra, a partial incarnation of Vishnu.

SHIGHRAGA. A king in the line of Ikshvaku, son of Agnivarna and father of Maru.

SHIVA. The god who destroys the universe at the end of the world. The Lord of Yogis, Uma's consort. Also known as Sthanu, Mahadeva, Maheshwara, Bhava.

SHRUTIKIRTI. The wife of Shatrughan, daughter of King Kushadvaja.

SHUDRA. The servant caste.

SHUKA. A rakshasa, a messenger of Ravan.

SHUKRADEVA. A sage.

SHUNASHEPHA. Son of Richika, a human sacrifice in King Ambarisha's aswamedha rite.

SHURPANKHA. A rakshasi, sister of Ravan.

SIDDHA. Accomplished yogis with supernatural powers.

SIDDHA ASHRAM. The ashram where Vāmana inscribed the universe in three strides.

SIDDHARTHA. A minister of King Dasharatha.

SIDDHI. A supernatural power attained through yogic feats.

SINGHIKA. A demoness in the ocean who killed her prey by catching their shadows.

SITA. Consort of Ram, daughter of King of Mithila, King Janak. A divine incarnation of Lakshmi. Also known as Janaki, Vaidehi, Maithili.

SKANDA. The son of Shiva. Also known as Karttik. The commander-in-chief of the god's army.

SOMADA. A gandharvi and mother of Brahmadatta who conceived by thought and maintained her chastity.

SON OF BHRIGU. Parasuram.

SON OF GĀDHI. One of the names of Vishwamitra.

SRI RAM. An avatar of Vishnu. One of the names of Ram (see Ram).

SRI GANGA. The Ganges, see GANGA.

SRI. One of the names of Lakshmi devi.

SUBAHU. A rakshasa who disturbed the sacrifice of sage Vishwamitra.

SUDARSHAN. A king in the line of Ikshvaku, son of Pravridha and father of Shankhan.

SUDHRITI. A king in the line of Nimi, son of Mahavir and father of Dhrishtaketu.

SUGRIVA. The king of the banars and younger brother to Bāli. Ram's friend and devotee.

SUKESHA. A rakshasa favored by Lord Shiva.

SUKETU. A king in the line of Nimi, son of Nandivardhan and father of Devarata. Also the name of a yakshas, father of Tāṭakā.

SUMALI. A rakshasa, son of Sukesha, brother of Malyavan and Mali.

SUMANTRA. Dasharatha's trusted minister.

SUMATI. Queen of King Sagar and mother of sixty-thousand sons.

SUMITRA. One of Dasharatha's queens. The mother of Lakshman and Shatrughan.

SUNDA. The husband of Tāṭakā, son of Jambha.

SUNDARA KĀṆḌA. The section of the Ramayana that describes Hanuman's search in Lanka for Sita.

SUPARSHIWA. A raptor, Sampāti's son.

SURSA. A rakshasi, Mother of the Snakes.

SURYA. The sun.

SUSAMDHI. A king in the line of Ikshvaku, son of Mandhata and father of Dhruvasamdhi.

SUSHENA. A general in the banar tribe, father of Tārā.

SUTIKSHNA. A saint.

SUVELA MOUNTAIN. A mountain on Lanka.

SUYAJNA. A sage.

SVARNAROMA. A king in the line of Nimi, son of Maharoma and father of Hrasvaroma.

SWAMI. A sage or monk.

SWAYAMPRABHA. A female ascetic.

SWAYAMBHU. Brahma, the creator of the universe.

TAMASĀ. Name of a river.

TAPASYA. Tapas, austerity, or practice of self-discipline.

TĀRĀ. The main queen of Bāli. Also, one of the banar generals.

TĀṬAKĀ. A yakshini, mother of Maricha.

THREE-EYED LORD. One of the names of Shiva (see SHIVA).

TRETA YUG. The age where dharma is diminished by one-fourth.

TRIJATA. A brahmin.

TRIPATHAGA. A name of the River Ganges.

TRISHANKU. A king in the line of Ikshvaku, son of Prithu and father of Yuvanashva, who wanted to ascend heaven in his human form.

TRISHIRĀ. A demon with three heads that was killed by Ram. Also the name of a rakshasa son of Ravan.

TRYAMBAKA. One of the names of Shiva (see SHIVA).

TUMBURU. A gandharva who was cursed by Kuvera to become a demon and was liberated from the curse by Ram.

UDAVASU. A king in the line of Nimi, son of Janaka and father of Nandivardhan.

UMA. Consort of Shiva and daughter of Himavat. Also known as Parvati.

URMILA. The wife of Lakshman, daughter of King Janak.

URVASHI. A celestial nymph.

UTTARA KĀṆDA. The section of the Ramayana that describes the part of Ram's life after he returned to Ayodhya from exile.

VAIDEHI. One of the names of Sita (see SITA). Daughter of Videha, King of Mithila.

VAIKUṆṬHA. Lord Vishnu's abode.

VAISHRAVANA. The brother of Ravan, grandson of Pulastya, son of Vishrava, the Guardian of Wealth.

VAJRADAMSHTRA. A rakshasa in Ravan's army.

VALMIKI. A rishi who is the author of the Ramayana.

VĀMANA. An incarnation of Vishnu as a dwarf.

VARAHA. A mountain in the sea.

VARUNA. Lord of the Waters.

VARUNI. Daughter of Varuna, also known as wine.

VASHISHTHA. A divine sage, brahmarishi. One of the mind-born sons of Brahma. The family priest of Dasharatha.

VĀSUKI. King of Snakes.

VATSAS. A river across the Ganges.

VAYU. The God of Air, the God of the Wind, Maruta, father of Hanuman.

VEDAVATI. A female ascetic who cursed Ravan that she would be the cause of his death in another lifetime.

VIBHĀNDAKA. A sage, son of Kashyap and father of Rishyashringa.

VIBUDHA. A king in the line of Nimi, son of Devamidha and father of Mahidraka.

VIDYUTKESHA. A rakshasa, son of Heti.

VIKUKSHI. Son of Kukshi, father of Bāna, a king in the line of Ikshvaku.

VINATA. A banar warrior.

VINDHYA MOUNTAIN. A range of mountains in southern India.

VIRĀDHA. A demon who was slain by Ram who was previously the gandharva Tumburu.

VIRUPAKSHA. A rakshasa in Ravan's army.

VISHĀLĀ. A city on the banks of the Ganges.

VISHNU. The god who sustains the universe.

VISHRAVA. A sage, the son of Pulastya, and father of Vaishravana and Ravan.

VISHVAKARMA. The divine architect.

VISHWAMITRA. A sage who attained brahminhood through austerity.

VIVASVAT. The sun god, son of Kashyap.

VRITRA. A brahmin daitya who was slain by Indra.

YADU. The son of Yayāti.

YAKSHA. The sacrificers, attendants on Kuvera, non-human beings.

YAKSHINI. A female demon.

YAMA. The Lord of Death.

YAMUNA. A river that meets the Ganges.

YANTRA. A sacred geometrical design.

YAYĀTI. A king in the line of Ikshvaku, son of Nahusha and father of Aja.

YUDDHA KĀNDA. The part of the Ramayana that describes the war between Ram and Ravan, the banar force and the demon force.

YUDDHONMATTA. A rakshasa, brother of Ravan.

YUDHAJIT. The brother of Queen Kaikeyi.

YUVANASHVA. A king in the line of Ikshvaku, son of Trishanku and father of Mandhata.

Recommended Reading

Although there are many English translations of the *Ramayana*, the following are most helpful.

Buck, William. *Ramayana*. Berkeley: University of California Press, 1981.

Chinmayananda, Swami, and Kumari Bharathi Naik. *Bala Ramayanam*. Madras: Chinmaya Publications Trust.

Das, Abinas Chandra. *Rgvedic India*. Delhi: Motilal Banarsidas, 1971.

Griffith, T.H. *The Ramayan of Valmiki*. Varanasi: The Chowkhamba Sanskrit Series Office, 1963.

Keshavadas, Sadguru Sant. *Ramayana At A Glance*. Lakemont, GA: CSA Printing & Bindery, Inc., 1976.

Menen, Aubrey. *The Ramayana*. New York: Charles Scribner's Sons, 1954.

Narayan, R.K. *The Ramayana*. New York: The Viking Press, 1972.

Raghavacharya, T. Srinivasa. *Gems From Ramayana*. Bombay: Bharatiya Vidya Bhavan, 1961.

Raghavan, V. *The Greater Ramayan*. Varanasi: The All-India Kashiraj Trust, 1973.

Rajagopalachari, C. *Ramayana*. Bombay: Bharatiya Vidya Bhavan, 1975.

Sen, Makhan Lal. *The Ramayana of Valmiki*. New Delhi: Munshiram Manoharlal Publishers Pvt. Ltd., 1978.

Sharma, Ramashraya. *A Socio-Political Study of the Valmiki Ramayana*. Delhi: Motilal Banarsidas, 1971.

Shastri, Hari Prasad, (Trans.) *The Ramayana of Valmiki*. Vol. I, II, III. London: Shantisudan, 1962.

Srimad Valmiki Ramayana, Parts I and II. Gorakpur: Gita Press, 1974.

Subramaniam, Kamala. *Ramayana*. Bombay: Bharatiya Vidya Bhavan, 1990.

Venkatesananda, Swami. *The Concise Ramayana of Valmiki*. Albany: State University of New York Press, 1988.

ABOUT THE AUTHOR

Yogi, scientist, philosopher, humanitarian, and mystic poet, Swami Rama is the founder and spiritual head of the Himalayan International Institute of Yoga Science and Philosophy, with its headquarters in Honesdale, Pennsylvania, and therapy and educational centers throughout the world. He was born in a Himalayan valley of Uttar Pradesh, India, in 1925 and was initiated and anointed in early childhood by a great sage of the Himalayas. He studied with many adepts, and then traveled to Tibet to study with his grandmaster. From 1949 to 1952 he held the respected position of Shankaracharya (spiritual leader) in Kirvirpitham in the South of India. He then returned to the Himalayas to intensify his meditative practices in the cave monasteries and to establish an ashram in Rishikesh.

Later, he continued his investigation of Western psychology and philosophy at several European universities, and he taught in Japan before coming to the United States in 1969. The following year he served as a consultant to the Voluntary Controls Project of the Research Department of the Menninger Foundation. There he demonstrated, under laboratory conditions, precise control over his autonomic nervous system and brain. The findings of that research increased the scientific community's understanding of the human ability to control autonomic functioning and to attain previously unrecognized levels of consciousness.

Shortly thereafter, Swami Rama founded the Himalayan Institute as a means to synthesize the ancient teachings of the East with the modern approaches of the West. He has played a major role in bringing the insights of yoga psychology and philosophy to the attention of the physicians and psychologists of the West. He continues to teach students around the world, and is the author of more than two dozen books.

The Himalayan Institute

Since its establishment in 1971, the Himalayan Institute has been dedicated to helping individuals develop themselves physically, mentally, and spiritually, as well as contributing to the transformation of society. All the Institute programs—educational, therapeutic, research—emphasize holistic health, yoga, and meditation as tools to help achieve those goals. Institute programs combine the best of ancient wisdom and modern science, of Eastern teachings and Western technologies. We invite you to join with us in this ongoing process of personal growth and development.

Our beautiful national headquarters, on a wooded, 400-acre campus in the Pocono Mountains of northeastern Pennsylvania, provides a peaceful, healthy setting for our seminars, classes, and training programs in the principles and practices of holistic living. Students from around the world have joined us here for the past fifteen years to attend programs in such diverse areas as biofeedback and stress reduction, hatha yoga, meditation, diet and nutrition, philosophy and metaphysics, and practical psychology for better living. We see the realization of our human potentials as a lifelong quest, leading to increased health, creativity, happiness, awareness, and improving the quality of life.

The Institute is a nonprofit organization. Your membership in the Institute helps to support its programs. Please call or write for information on becoming a member.

Institute Programs, Services, and Facilities

All Institute programs share an emphasis on conscious, holistic living and personal self-development. You may enjoy any of a number of diverse programs, including:

- Special weekend or extended seminars to teach skills and techniques for increasing your ability to be healthy and enjoy life
- Holistic health services
- Professional training for health professionals
- Meditation retreats and advanced meditation instruction
- Cooking and nutritional training
- Hatha yoga and exercise workshops
- Residential programs for self-development

The Himalayan Institute Charitable Hospital

A major aspect of the Institute's work around the world is its construction and management of a modern, comprehensive hospital and holistic health facility in the mountain area of Dehra Dun, India. Outpatient facilities are already providing medical care to those in need, and mobile units have been equipped to visit outlying villages. Construction work on the main hospital building is progressing as scheduled.

We welcome financial support to help with the construction and the provision of services. We also welcome donations of medical supplies, equipment, or professional expertise. If you would like further information on the Hospital, please contact us.

Himalayan Institute Publications

Art of Joyful Living	Swami Rama
Book of Wisdom (Ishopanishad)	Swami Rama
A Call to Humanity	Swami Rama
Celestial Song/Gobind Geet	Swami Rama
Choosing a Path	Swami Rama
The Cosmic Drama: Bichitra Natak	Swami Rama
Enlightenment Without God	Swami Rama
Exercise Without Movement	Swami Rama
Freedom from the Bondage of Karma	Swami Rama
Indian Music, Volume I	Swami Rama
Inspired Thoughts of Swami Rama	Swami Rama
Japji: Meditation in Sikhism	Swami Rama
Lectures on Yoga	Swami Rama
Life Here and Hereafter	Swami Rama
Living with the Himalayan Masters	Swami Rama
Love and Family Life	Swami Rama
Love Whispers	Swami Rama
Meditation and Its Practice	Swami Rama
Path of Fire and Light, Vol. I	Swami Rama
Path of Fire and Light, Vol. II	Swami Rama
Perennial Psychology of the Bhagavad Gita	Swami Rama
A Practical Guide to Holistic Health	Swami Rama
Sukhamani Sahib: Fountain of Eternal Joy	Swami Rama
The Valmiki Ramayana Retold in Verse	Swami Rama
The Wisdom of the Ancient Sages	Swami Rama
Creative Use of Emotion	Swami Rama, Swami Ajaya
Science of Breath	Swami Rama, Rudolph Ballentine, M.D., Alan Hymes, M.D.
Yoga and Psychotherapy	Swami Rama, Rudolph Ballentine, M.D., Swami Ajaya, Ph.D.
The Mystical Poems of Kabir	Swami Rama, Robert Regli
Yoga-sutras of Patanjali	Usharbudh Arya, D.Litt.
Superconscious Meditation	Usharbudh Arya, D.Litt.
Mantra and Meditation	Usharbudh Arya, D.Litt.
Philosophy of Hatha Yoga	Usharbudh Arya, D.Litt.
Meditation and the Art of Dying	Usharbudh Arya, D.Litt.
God	Usharbudh Arya, D.Litt.
Psychotherapy East and West	Swami Ajaya, Ph.D.
Yoga Psychology	Swami Ajaya, Ph.D.

Psychology East and West	Swami Ajaya, Ph.D. (ed.)
Diet and Nutrition	Rudolph Ballentine, M.D.
Joints and Glands Exercises	Rudolph Ballentine, M.D. (ed.)
Transition to Vegetarianism	Rudolph Ballentine, M.D.
Theory and Practice of Meditation	Rudolph Ballentine, M.D. (ed.)
Freedom from Stress	Phil Nuernberger, Ph.D.
Science Studies Yoga	James Funderburk, Ph.D.
Homeopathic Remedies	Dale Buegel, M.D., Blair Lewis, P.A.-C, Dennis Chernin, M.D., M.P.H.
Hatha Yoga Manual I	Samskrti and Veda
Hatha Yoga Manual II	Samskrti and Judith Franks
Seven Systems of Indian Philosophy	Rajmani Tigunait, Ph.D.
The Tradition of the Himalayan Masters	Rajmani Tigunait, Ph.D.
Yoga on War and Peace	Rajmani Tigunait, Ph.D.
Swami Rama of the Himalayas	L.K. Misra, Ph.D. (ed.)
Sikh Gurus	K.S. Duggal
Philosophy and Faith of Sikhism	K.S. Duggal
The Quiet Mind	John Harvey, Ph.D. (ed.)
Himalayan Mountain Cookery	Martha Ballentine
The Yoga Way Cookbook	Himalayan Institute
Meditation in Christianity	Himalayan Institute
Art and Science of Meditation	Himalayan Institute
Inner Paths	Himalayan Institute
Chants from Eternity	Himalayan Institute
Spiritual Diary	Himalayan Institute
Blank Books	Himalayan Institute

To order or to request a free mail order catalog call or write
The Himalayan Publishers
RR 1, Box 400
Honesdale, PA 18431
Toll-free 1-800-822-4547